MARKETING
TO THE
SOCIAL WEB

MARKETING
TO THE
SOCIAL WEB

How Digital Customer Communities Build Your Business

SECOND EDITION

LARRY WEBER

WILEY

John Wiley & Sons, Inc.

For general information on our other products and services or for technical support, please contact our Customer Care Department within the United States at (800) 762-2974, outside the United States at (317) 572-3993 or fax (317) 572-4002.

Wiley also publishes its books in a variety of electronic formats. Some content that appears in print may not be available in electronic books. For more information about Wiley products, visit our web site at www.wiley.com.

ISBN: 978-0470-41097-4

Printed in the United States of America.

10 9 8 7 6 5 4 3

For Hannah, Julia and Geoffrey
. . . may your lives always be a
'verb thing, not a noun thing'

CONTENTS

PART III
MAKING USE OF THE FOUR ONLINE CONDUIT STRATEGIES

FOREWORD

You may have heard Jimmy say his now famous phrase, "Imagine a world in which every person on the planet is given free access to the sum of all human knowledge. That's what we're doing." Had it not been for an important change in direction eight years ago, that phrase would never have been uttered.

The predecessor to Wikipedia was actually the free encyclopedia Nupedia, which was built upon the traditional peer-review model of academic research. In other words, a traditional approval and gate-keeping process was very much in place. And while Nupedia saw some growth during its two-year existence, it wasn't until the idea of opening up the contribution of content to everyone, and using a wiki platform to do so, that Wikipedia was born. What has made Wikipedia a global phenomenon is the idea that anyone interested in participating certainly can, which has given rise to a previously unprecedented collaboration based on a sense of ownership and community among thousands of volunteer contributors around the world.

Was it sheer luck that Wikipedia achieved its global success? Certainly historical timing was a benefit. But what really happened is that Jimmy and his employee Larry Sanger realized the old model of top-down uni-directional communication wasn't working anymore and that people were really looking for a sense of community and a voice.

When it comes right down to it, humans haven't fundamentally changed since their evolutionary ancestors first walked the earth—they've thrived on interaction and connection, namely community. It's this concept—the need for community—that Larry Weber drives home in *Marketing to the Social Web*. Weber understands what the new marketing is all about, which is not selling, per se. The end goal might be a sale or something similar, but in reality it's community and engagement that get people interested.

In this book, Weber helps marketers, whose job ultimately it is to introduce products and services to people who are sincerely interested in them, learn how to do it the right way. In chapter after chapter, he drives home the point that you can't fake sincerity, you can't fake authenticity, and you can't fake caring because the consumers, users, or participants that marketers are hoping to attract will smell any poser-like behavior a mile away. He accurately points out that "a brand is actually a living, changing thing, [and] is based on the dialogue you have with your customers and prospects—the stronger the dialogue, the stronger the brand, the weaker the dialogue, the weaker the brand."

So, while this is a marketing book with many practical tips, its underlying principle is respect for customers and consumers. For example, Weber encourages marketers that "when you start or join a social web conversation about your company or your competitors, you should be up-front about who you are."

Without being preachy, he also emphasizes the rise of branding and moral purpose on the web: "[Moral purpose] means offering value and acting ethically and transparently. . . . The ethics around doing business include: environmental responsibility, diversity in employment, considering the larger effects of the company's actions. . . . you need to have moral purpose embedded in your values, along with great products at a great price."

For marketers still somewhat unfamiliar—and perhaps uncomfortable—with the new rules of effective online engagement, particularly when it comes to measuring success, he offers practical suggestions such as looking at a blend of quantifiable and qualitative measures like share of voice, level of engagement, tone of discourse, evidence/quality of community, cost of market share and such things as how frequently and in what manner an organization is being discussed online, among other things.

Ultimately, *Marketing to the Social Web* is an excellent blend of theory, practical tips and how-tos, and fun and interesting case studies that will serve both marketers new to the Web and those more seasoned, making it a timely read for everyone interested in growing and thriving online.

—Jimmy Wales, founder of Wikipedia
and Andrea Weckerle, Communications
Consultant & Entrepreneur, New York City

PREFACE

In late 1993, I received a phone call from Michael Dertouzos, the founder and head of MIT's Laboratory for Computer Science. He said he wanted to see me for two reasons; first, to help promote the extraordinary innovations coming out of the lab, and second, to discuss the marketing of the recent work of a young British researcher who was moving to the lab from a stint at CERN (the Organisation Européenne pour la Recherche Nucléaire) in Switzerland.

A few days later, the larger-than-life Michael and a quiet Tim Berners-Lee were sitting in my Cambridge office. Michael spoke of the many things the lab had accomplished and the work in progress. He showed me a videotape of his 1980 appearance on the *Today* show to discuss the impact of the first personal computers on society. The interviewer pushed Michael to agree that the advent of the PC was just a fad, but Michael politely disagreed and went on to describe a world in which a large digital community would soon be formed by connecting all personal commuters so that people could easily communicate, shop, learn—even get advice from physicians on another continent. The interviewer just shook his head and broke for a commercial.

Then it was Tim's turn. He discussed his recent work, the development of a language called html—hypertext markup language—that he planned to layer onto the Internet to create a World Wide Web. He asked if I thought the name was catchy, and I smiled, because I really had no idea what he was talking about.

Michael explained he was forming the World Wide Web Consortium and he wanted us to help promote and educate the world. Now, some 16 years later, we still have not seen the full impact of this most important innovation of our lifetimes. Michael left us too early, and Bill Gates, to whom Michael often consulted on a variety of topics about the future, called his passing a major loss in one major newsweekly. Tim, now Sir Tim, continues to work on his next phase, the semantic web, and I heeded Michael's advice to study the marketing implications of the Web.

The Web has and will continue to change everything. A world of transparent content, mostly user-generated, broadband, rich media, and available on multiple devices, continues to evolve. Marketing at its best is the influencing of opinion through compelling content; doing so through the Web will get harder before it gets easier, but the change is gaining momentum. The Web has consumed almost all the traditional media: television, print, radio, and direct mail and will make marketing a set of dialogues. Companies will have to learn to contribute to these dialogues and share with their customers and potential customers. I've written this book to suggest how you can do just that.

—Larry Weber, Buenos Aires

PREFACE TO THE SECOND EDITION

In the 18 months since the first edition of this book was published, more and more companies have learned to stimulate and maintain dialogues with their customers and prospects on the social web. I would like to think that the first edition of this book has helped a good number of executives to think about ways to do so. But since the social web is evolving so rapidly with new tools, techniques, and opportunities, the book demanded a new edition to stay current.

This second edition has an additional chapter on the Facebook phenomenon and how marketers can use it. I've completely rewritten the chapters on blogs and measurements, and updated examples and illustrations in every chapter. To obtain the most current thinking about marketing to the social web, I've interviewed several more executives and quoted the most current research available.

Fortunately, the principles of marketing have not changed, so any marketing executive can read and apply the ideas in this edition. Those who do so will, I believe, have stronger brands, products, services, and customer relationships than those who dismiss the social web as just one more fad of the times.

—Larry Weber,
Waltham, MA

ACKNOWLEDGMENTS

First and foremost I must thank my phenomenal co-writer Wally Wood, who truly understood my goals, thinking, and organization around this important book, as well as our earlier book, *The Provocateur*. These books would not have happened without his skillful hand. Thanks to Marijean Lauzier for always supporting my visionary discretions. Jackie Lustig, Jan Baxter, Brian Cavoli, Kevin Green and all at W2 Group who gave freely of their time and talents to bring this book to fruition while making my "second" career such a joy.

Reid Hoffman (LinkedIn.com), Diane Hessan (Communispace), John Palfrey, (Berkman Center for Internet & Society), Tom Gerace (Gather.com), Don McLagan, (Compete.com), Dan Morrison, (ITtoolbox.com), Josh Scribner (IBM Corporate Communications), Stuart Brotman (American Television Experience), Jerry Swerling (Annenberg School for Communication at USC at Los Angeles), Judy Strauss (U of N, Reno), David Berkowitz (360i.com), Jim Nail (TNS Cymfony.com), Marcel Lebrun (Radian6.com), Bob Walczak (Ringleader.com), Dan Bruns (Mzinga.com), Elisa Camahort Page (BlogHer.com), Jeremy Allaire (Brightcove.com), John Lawn (Food Management), and Ethan Beard (Facebook.com) all gave of their time but, more importantly, their deepest thinking on the social web. I am forever indebted to them, as I am to the many clients and former clients, and the large group of academics, authors, politicians, and executives who freely engaged in numerous conversations that helped shape my thinking.

I thank my agent Jill Kneerim and my editor, Richard Narramore, whose subtle, but swift and clear touch has made this book a very good read. Also to all the great people at John Wiley & Sons, Inc., including Tiffany Groglio and Lauren Freestone, who made the "process" of turning words into this book as painless as possible.

Finally, and as always, I want to thank my family, especially Dawn, for their support and love of a dreamer businessman who wants to help good businesses become great.

Pandemonium: The Landscape of the Social Web

The Web Is Not a Channel

(And You're an Aggregator, not a Broadcaster)

L earning to market to the social web requires learning a new way to communicate with an audience in a digital environment. It's that simple.

It does not require executives to forget everything they know about marketing. It does mean that they have to open their minds to new possibilities, social change, and rethinking past practices. In the pages ahead, I look at what we can learn about these new possibilities and what the *social web* is all about.

Instead of continuing as broadcasters, marketers should—and will—become aggregators of customer communities. Rather than broadcasting marketing messages to an increasingly indifferent, even resentful, audience jaded by the 2,000-plus messages the average American is reportedly exposed to every day, marketers should participate in, organize, and encourage social networks to which people want to belong. Rather than talking *at* customers, marketers should talk *with* them. And the social web is the most effective way in the history of the world to do just that on a large scale.

The social web is the online place where people with a common interest can gather to share thoughts, comments, and opinions. It includes social networks such as MySpace, Gather, Facebook, BlackPlanet, Eons, LinkedIn, and hundreds (actually, as we'll see, hundreds of thousands) more. It includes branded web destinations like Amazon, Netflix, and eBay. It includes enterprise sites such as IBM, Best Buy, Cisco, and Oracle. The social web is a new world of unpaid media created by individuals or enterprises on the web. These new strategies, which have the capacity to change public opinion every hour—if not every minute—include:

Reputation aggregators are search engines such as Google, Yahoo!, Ask, and Live. They aggregate sites with the best product or service to offer and usually put things in order of reputation. Mobile search is increasingly popular as people on the go check for a nearby restaurant, directions to a store, or the best price for a product.

Blogs are online journals where people can post ideas, images, and links to other web pages or sites. Some appear on personal or corporate sites, while others are hosted on Blogger, BlogHer (for women), Weblog, Tumblr, and other blogging sites. The micro-blog site Twitter, where users post "tweets" of 140 characters at a time, is another twist. Lenovo's web-marketing vice president says, "I use Twitter to monitor tweets about our brand—looking for people having a tough time with our products. I also see a lot of opportunity to sell through Twitter, and I expect we'll open a 'deal' channel there soon."[1]

Topic-specific e-communities are generally advertising supported although some are free. Business-oriented e-communities include dozens concerning IBM: for IBM interns, around different IBM products and services, etc.[2] Hewlett Packard has communities on its web site: an HP blade community and IT resource center forums.[3] There are interesting healthcare communities: Sermo for physicians and Patientslikeme, which has communities around specific diseases. There are communities involving sports such as KayakMind for people who enjoy kayaking.[4] Password-protected e-communities are growing especially quickly.

Social networks are places where people with a common interest or concern come together to meet people with similar interests, express themselves, and vent. In addition to the examples I've already cited, other social networks include iVillage, Xanga, and Stumbleupon. Dopplr is an interesting site for business travelers who share their experiences with foreign hotels, restaurants, and attractions; it will also tell you when, say, three people you know will be in Paris at the same time you are. Some sites are devoted specifically to image-sharing, open to the wide world or restricted to a select few through password protection. YouTube (now owned by Google) serves up 10 billion videos a month to U.S. viewers alone; photos and videos posted on Flickr (now owned by Yahoo!) attract more than 40 million visitors monthly.

In traditional publisher- or corporate-controlled media such as newspapers, magazines, radio, and television, the communication is overwhelmingly one way. Professional journalists research and write stories that are edited and disseminated to the public.

Social media such as blogs, however, allow everyone to publish and to participate in multithreaded conversations online. Because bloggers, sometimes referred to as "citizen journalists" or even "citizen marketers," have no editorial constraints and have access to the entire Web, their posts can make or break personal, product, or corporate reputations.

Online communities started in the early days of the Internet and software companies encouraged "user groups" to test and experiment with new programs. The Well in California, CompuServe, and America Online built on that idea and began to attract people to the Internet who didn't have a community or who felt somewhat on the fringe of the new social order, where the groups were a way to meet and bond with new people. As Reid Hoffman, the founder of LinkedIn.com, says, "It was almost like the frontier. Who were the people who originally went West? They felt they didn't really fit with this society; were somewhat alienated; and wanted to take a big risk. So they got in their wagons and headed West to make something happen. That's the reason why there was this fascination with things like chat rooms and message boards. Wow, you are with these people you don't know. Anonymity was a big part of this because it was like this Wild West kind of community."

Today, there are online tools to manage and present your identity, to communicate with people, to bring yourself online and make yourself heard. Today, individuals and organizations are founding Web-based communities at a mind-boggling pace. People are using the Web to find others with similar interests, to shop more efficiently, to learn about products and services, to vent about shoddy products and poor service, and to stay in touch with distant relatives and friends on the other side of the world.

As Microsoft CEO Steven A. Ballmer told the *New York Times*, "I think one pervasive change is the increasing importance of community. That will come in different forms, with different age groups of people, and it will change as the technology evolves. But the notion of multiple people interacting on things—that will forever continue. That's different today, and we're going to see those differences build. You see it in a variety of ways now, in social networking sites, in the way people collaborate at work, and in ad hoc collaboration over the Internet. You see it in things like Xbox Live, the way we let people come together and have community entertainment experiences. And you'll see that in TV and video. It's not like the future of entertainment has been determined. But it's a big deal."[5]

Here's an example of social media at work. When BMW relaunched the Mini Cooper in 2002, widespread publicity and unconventional promotions (online and off) generated lots of test drives and got car sales in gear. Not long ago, Mini's marketers spoofed the car-happy 1970s TV series *Starsky & Hutch* with *Hammer and Coop*, a series of six webisodes featuring car chases without ever mentioning the brand. To support the webisodes, they aired quirky movie trailers, dangled Minis off billboards, and cast the Mini as the star of fashion spreads in men's magazines.

Mini has been a web-savvy brand with attitude from the get-go. It's always packed its site with an ever-changing array of features: a build-your-own car configuration page; virtual factory tour; various games and screensavers; and special owners-only e-newsletters and community pages. Still, when the buzz started dying down, Mini's marketing manager knew she needed more than a sticky web site and intriguing ads to reignite it.

Mini hired MotiveQuest to analyze online conversations about the brand and its competitors by monitoring posts on blogs and social networks as well as on specialized sites like Yahoo Autos.

MotiveQuest's CEO, David Rabjohns, found that "Mini owners were not only talking about things like performance and handling but community type things like picture sharing, getting together at events, and personal etiquette, the Mini way." Not surprisingly, many posts involved non-Mini owners asking Mini owners about their experiences.

This analysis prompted Mini to ask its most enthusiastic supporters for help in rebuilding the buzz. Now the company invites bloggers to test drive new models and has a blogger who podcasts from special events like the cross-country "Mini Takes the States" festivals that bring thousands of brand fans (owners and non-owners alike) together for rallies, music, and more. The web site includes "Mini Mail" virtual postcards and other viral activities that let Mini fans get the conversation going in their own way.

Do more online conversations sell Minis? Trudy Hardy, Mini's marketing manager, says "we definitely see some correlation between online activity and how that affects showroom traffic. We look at the spikes that are going on in conversations and see if it measures against an increased amount of traffic to our site, which ultimately leads to an increased amount of leads we send to our dealers."[6]

I'd say the real value of social media here is in rebuilding the Mini's buzz and reinforcing the hip, non-mainstream attitude that distinguishes the brand from its rivals. Getting people to think "Mini" and talk to friends about the brand or check out the web site is more likely to steer them toward a purchase down the road.

Now take a quick look at what Dell is doing. You may remember the company was soundly blasted in the blogosphere for customer service problems. Today Dell is turning social media to its advantage by inserting itself into online conversations in a positive way. Dell aims to make 100 million additional customer contacts every year through blog posts, Twitter tweets, and brand-related e-communities. These contacts aren't directly sales-related—but they will help Dell start or keep conversations going with customers. Just as important, customers will have more opportunities to share information with each other and with Dell.

Of course, Mini and Dell are hardly the only companies learning to market to the social web. But they are harbingers of your future.

Pandemonium in Media and Markets

The marketing worlds are pandemonium these days. American consumers have more choices, more products, more services, more media, more messages, and more digital conversations than ever. Consider media:

- *Television.* Between cable and satellite, the average American household receives 70 or more television stations, a number that continues to grow, and the average time spent viewing continues to hold its own. Network TV and spot TV ad spending was down in 2007, however, even as prime-time broadcast TV product placements were up sharply.

- *Magazines.* Although publishers introduced more than 1,000 new magazines titles last year, the total number of titles, average magazine circulation, and single-copy sales continue to drift downward. National magazine advertising was up last year, but local magazine advertising went down.

- *Newspapers.* Newspaper circulation fell by 3 percent last year; in the past five years, it has dropped 8 percent, a plunge hastened by the Web. And advertising is following readers out the door, also dropping by 3 percent last year. Classified ads are shifting online to sites like Monster.com (jobs) and Craigslist.com (jobs and everything else). Small wonder that in a global survey of newspaper editors, 44 percent said most people will be getting their news online within 10 years (although judging by current trends, I'd say within five years, max).

- *Radio.* Satellite radio offers hundreds of channels of music, sports, news, and features, commentary, many of which are commercial-free. You don't want to listen to commercials? Subscribe to satellite radio. Meanwhile, network and spot radio ad spending are both down, according to Nielsen.

- *Internet.* As more people and companies log on and join the conversation, Internet advertising expenditures are going up, up, up. According to eMarketer, ad spending on U.S. social-networking sites increased 70% last year to $1.56 billion and will exceed $2 billion this year.[7]

New product marketing is also pandemonium, for example:

- According to the Food Institute, marketers introduced over 16,000 new food products last year (over 2,500 new beverages alone). They introduced over 13,000 nonfood products—including 4,230 new cosmetics, 2,793 new skin care items, and 1,259 new hair care products.

- Exhibitors at the International Consumer Electronics Show introduced more than 10,000 new audio, digital imaging/video, gaming, home theater, home networking, mobile, and wireless products.

- Exhibitors at the International Home and Housewares Show introduced another 10,000-plus new small kitchen appliances, kitchenware, bath and shower accessories, decorative accessories, and personal care appliances.

- Exhibitors at the National Hardware Show introduced another 5,000-plus new hardware, home, and garden items.

The list goes on: Exhibitors at the New York Auto Show introduced . . . Exhibitors at the Ft. Lauderdale International Boat Show . . . Exhibitors at the International Camping and Outdoor Show . . . but you get the idea—and this does not include business-to-business products and services. Or new pharmaceuticals and medical devices. Or travel opportunities . . . or educational offerings.

What's a marketer to do in this teeming mass of newnesses?

From Broadcasters to Aggregators

Before looking ahead, let's take a quick look back. Not so very long ago, marketers got the word out about their products or services in any way they could—newspaper and magazine ads, billboards, radio and television commercials. Each new medium added something. Magazines added color and national distribution to newspaper advertising. Billboards were in your face as you drove along the highways. Radio added sound and music. Television added movement and, even more than billboards or radio, intrusiveness.

Remember the days when the marketer controlled the message? About all television viewers could do was watch or get up to change channels (or go to the toilet), and for a good long time television advertising was incredibly effective. It still is for many products in many situations, but its very success brought about consumer reaction.

Today, 90 percent of the people who can avoid TV ads through TiVo, DVD recording, or the skip button on the VCR remote do so. In fact, only 18 percent of television advertising campaigns actually generate a positive return on the investment. And although total TV viewership has remained steady, new channels have fragmented the audience to such an extent that the broadcast networks NBC, CBS, and ABC have all lost audiences both relatively and absolutely.

Despite their shrinking audiences, these networks and other TV channels have continue to raise their ad rates; the cost per thousand (CPM) people reached of the average television commercial increased 265 percent between 1996 and 2005. CPMs continue to go up, even as the size of network audiences go down, so it's not surprising that

TV advertisers are unhappy. Some big spenders—Procter & Gamble, American Express, McDonald's—have begun experimenting with alternatives, but no major advertiser has decided to do something else.

It won't be news to you that most advertising is incredibly inefficient. When you advertise in mass media, you generally reach far more people than the potential customers you intend to reach. But as long as the CPMs were small, who cared? A certain amount of advertising waste was a cost of doing business.

True, marketers have tried to improve their advertising's efficiency. They've tried to match audience demographics—age, sex, education, income, household size—to their target market. For example, beer commercials appear in sports programs that young men tend to watch and disposable diaper commercials in daytime dramas that young mothers often watch. Still, demographics don't really work very well in trying to identify a target market for most products. Middle-aged and older men drink beer; fathers buy disposable diapers.

For 150 years or more, marketers, through newspapers, magazines, and then radio and television, have been broadcasting their messages to a potential market that they defined as well as they could. Advertisers have tried to put their ads in front of those prospective customers most likely to buy the company's product or service. But the goal has always been to reach as many people as possible with the hope that enough paying customers would respond to make the investment pay.

Today, sophisticated marketers realize that what worked in the past is not working (or not working well) now—and they need a new approach. As A.G. Lafley, the CEO of Procter & Gamble, told his executives, "We need to reinvent the way we market to consumers. We need a new model."

The Web Is Not a Channel

Steve Ballmer's observation hints at how thoroughly the social web will change our world. A century ago, although no one knew it at the time, the first automobile was not simply a self-propelled buggy. True, it got you from one place to another, but it also changed the face of the country, the design of cities. It changed courting behavior and where people could live and work. Similarly, television was not simply radio with pictures. By showing ordinary people in Eastern Europe and in the Soviet Union the lives of people in the West, television affected history. By showing Americans the Vietnam War in living color, television changed American society.

The Web will have as profound an effect on society as the automobile or television. In fact, we're only beginning to glimpse the Web's implications. For instance, the Web undoes some of the effects of 50 years of television. Remember how, in the early days of television, the ads and many programs showed the happy family—dad, mom, son, and sis—sitting together in front of the living room television? Today the reality is more like dad, mom, son, and sis all watching their own sets in separate rooms, if they are watching TV at all. Rather than bringing people together, television has, in many senses, brought about more isolation. People are home alone even if others are in the house; it is easier to click on the TV than go out to a bowling league, lodge night, or card game with the girls. In contrast, the social web, through the dialogue it encourages, is beginning to bring people together.

Since the dawn of the television age, the message of virtually all commercials has been: Buy! Buy! Buy! The unspoken contract was: Somebody's got to pay for your news, entertainment, and diversion and that's advertising, so Buy! Buy! Buy Now! Broadly speaking, for the past 60 years, most marketers have debated how to use television, radio, print, public relations, direct marketing, the Internet, and customer retention programs. What is the best medium to reach our market? What are our customers reading, watching, listening to? How can we attract their attention, stop them from turning the page or changing the channel? How can we best tell them about our product, our service, our benefits, our value?

For the past 10 years, corporations have been trained that they should use all the different media—newspapers, magazines, direct mail, television, public relations, and then the Internet. But the Internet is becoming the umbrella. Managers have to understand that the Web is rapidly becoming the most important marketing medium.

If you are a corporate marketer, you don't just drop some ads onto web sites the way you have dropped 30-second spots into television shows or a color spread into a magazine. A symptom of how things are changing: nearly every commercial during the Super Bowl is designed to send viewers to a digital destination.

People don't want to be sold. They are doing their best to avoid commercials. They have pop-up blockers to screen out the ads on the Web that are a distraction. Early Web advertisers, who saw the medium as just another advertising channel, treated it like a magazine ad equipped with sound and motion. But banner ads and pop-ups are not the best way to market on the Web.

People do want news and information about the things they care about—and they want it right now. One recent midnight, a friend's dog tangled with a skunk for the first time. She had no tomato juice, the traditional folk bath for a skunked dog. Five minutes on the Web, however, and she'd found a formula that included hydrogen peroxide and liquid dish detergent that she could mix up and de-stink the dog.

Community building—with communities focusing on a specific common interest—is one of the fastest growing applications on the Web. Examples include: ITtoolbox.com, where information technology professionals swap opinions on technology products and services; BootsnAll.com, where budget travelers share advice about, say, the best hotels in Katmandu; iVillage.com, where women trade ideas about diet and fitness, love and sex, home and food; HealthBoards. com, which has subgroups on 140 diseases that serve as forums for people to share experiences and discuss problems or new discoveries; and LinkedIn.com, where professionals go to network. All of this means that the Web is continuing to evolve.

Four Generations of the Web

During the first phase of the Web, 1990–1995, the focus was HTML and site building. I was present at the beginning. My experience with the Internet began in 1989–1990 when Michael Dertouzos, then the director of MIT's Laboratory for Computer Science, asked me to help promote the lab. It had developed a number of groundbreaking technologies—from RSA security to the spreadsheet to Ethernet—and Michael had successfully recruited Tim Berners-Lee to work on HTML at MIT. I helped lead the announcement of the World Wide Web Consortium based on the development of HTML.

We did early work for America Online (AOL), helping them establish and market early communities, then called chat rooms. The popular ones were for breast cancer survivors, Boston Red Sox fans, and personal finance. We helped Monster.com build its community, and in the mid-1990s, we launched E-GM for General Motors, one of the first automotive communities.

I've been deeply involved in many software and technology companies over the past 25 years such as Verizon Wireless, Hewlett Packard, Lotus Development, and Red Hat. I helped found the largest interactive trade group in the country, Massachusetts Innovation and Technology Exchange, which is now 12 years old, with almost 10,000 members. And during this time, I've watched the Internet evolve.

With the advent of the browser, the second phase involved more interactivity and transactional things, search, click-throughs, and pop-ups. That phase lasted 10 years and has now given way to the third phase: the rise of the social web, all the things I have been describing and will be talking about in detail in the chapters ahead.

Web 4.0, which is right around the corner, will feature rich media (full of video, sound, even touch) and broadband, with high definition making the Web more emotive. How does this work? Consider the growing popularity of video conferencing. For instance, at a Halo center, where the next generation of video-conferencing technology is in place, participants see three-dimensional, full-size, video conferencing; it's almost as if the people are in the same room and sharing the same experience. That is an example of rich media in action. The emotive element will include both personal and business sensations, the idea is that the experiences offer not only emotions—joy, curiosity, disgust, happiness—but also, on the business side, sensations of satisfaction and fulfillment.

In this new world, the customer is in control. There are still only 24 hours in a day, and if people become more involved with the Web, they're not going to have as much time to watch television, they're not going to listen to the radio, and they're not going to read the newspaper or a magazine. Publishers know this and are doing their best to create web sites that can supplement (or replace) their paper publications.

The real job of the marketer in the social web is to aggregate customers. You aggregate customers two ways: (1) by providing compelling content on your web site and creating retail environments that customers want to visit, and (2) by going out and participating in the public arena. If you are in the energy business, you should be participating in the energy blogosphere. If you are a pharmaceutical manufacturer, you should be participating in discussions about disease and its treatment. If you are a small fly rod maker, you should be participating in discussions about fly fishing.

Note that you do not have to be a *Fortune* 500 corporation to participate in these conversations. Indeed, it may be easier and more effective for a relatively small or medium-size company to take maximum advantage of the principles I lay out in this book.

The social web will be the most critical marketing environment around. Much the way newspapers were critical in the 1800s, magazines and radio were critical in the first half of the twentieth century, and television was critical in the second half, the Internet began to become significant in the 1990s. It is rapidly growing more and more critical to marketing, but has shifted into a social digital space that I am calling the social web.

The social web will become the primary center of activity for whatever you do when you shop, plan, learn, or communicate. It may not take over your entire life (one hopes), but it will be the first place you turn for news, information, entertainment, diversion—all of the things that the older media supplied. In fact, according to a Forrester Research Report, young people (18–22) spend more time using a PC at home—10.7 hours a week—than they spend watching TV—10.2 hours a week—an important point for businesses looking to build early brand loyalty.[8]

Marketing, therefore, has to wrap around the social web, because what is truly changing in the social web is media, and marketing has always had to shape itself around media. Individuals and companies are becoming media. As you produce content, you become a medium. Now user-generated content—a key aspect of the social web—is bridging media. Just one of hundreds of examples: The retailer Cabela's, which sells outdoor products, features customer-contributed reviews and ratings in its catalogs, e-mail campaigns, and stores.

How do you market in this new environment? Ultimately, marketing disappears if it does its job right, because marketers become purveyors of an environment. A manager of an environment helps people make decisions to buy. That is the commercial and modernization side of things. A good example is how the brilliant chairman of Starbucks, Howard Schultz, and his people keep thinking about how they can enrich the Starbucks environment without turning people away. They've brought in music . . . some social causes . . . and Wi-Fi. Now think about how you can create digital experiences that encourages your customers to come back for more. There is pandemonium around the social web, like anything in its first phases, but it will self-organize.

It is important to understand that although we are at the beginning of the social web, marketers should dive in *now*. If you wait much longer, your competitors will have figured out how to attract your customers to their environments. If that happens, you will have to work three times as hard to get them back. Customers have only so much time. And if they're happy where they are, then they're less likely to leave.

A business friend started and runs a large retail clothing chain. When I saw him not long ago and asked how thing were going, he told me, "Well, good. My core loyal customers of the past 20 years are still core loyal customers. But when I go into the stores, I notice they're all starting to look older. Where are the younger people?" I suggested that they might be on SmartBargains.com or another clothing site. My friend had never heard of it.

Unless there's a change, my friend's chain will reach the proverbial tipping point; suddenly there are no customers in the stores at all. If that chain (or any retailer) does not get involved in social media and marketing, it will lose a whole generation of customers. They simply won't come to stores. They want a dialogue with your business, want to know you are there and available 24/7. Branding in the social web is the dialogue you have with your customer. The stronger the dialogue, the stronger your brand; the weaker the dialogue, the weaker your brand. You can easily find examples of great brands that lost their dialogue at one time or another: SONY, Disney, Coke, McDonald's.

Transparency is critical if you want customers and stakeholders to trust you and engage in dialogue with you. Doesn't it make sense that a CEO should mention his title (or at least use his real name) when blogging about his company or a company he's trying to acquire? John Mackey, CEO of Whole Foods, touched off quite a controversy when he used the alias *Rahodeb* to post notes on Yahoo! stock message boards. Rahodeb had lots of positive things to say about Whole Foods but not-so-nice comments about competitor (and acquisition target) Wild Oats Markets. "I think he looks cute!" Rahodeb wrote when someone made fun of Mackey's photo in the Whole Foods annual report. On the other hand, Rahodeb bashed Wild Oats, writing that its management "clearly doesn't know what it is doing."[9]

When the posts came to light and regulators raised concerns about the possibility that Rahodeb's comments might have affected the stock prices of Whole Foods and Wild Oats, Mackey apologized and stopped blogging. The SEC investigated and ultimately closed the case without taking any action. Later, the CEO explained the posts to the *Boston Globe* this way: "I participate in a number of online communities—pretty much anything I'm interested in. The thing I'm most interested in the world is Whole Foods. Plus, a large percentage of posters on a board like that are people that have an ax to grind. Whole Foods is my child. And here was my child being abused by all these vicious people. Almost all of my posts were responses that I made to lies and attacks that people had about Whole Foods. I defended Whole Foods. Somebody had to. That's really how I saw it."[10]

Here's how I see it: The lack of transparency is very troubling. When you start or join a social web conversation about your company or your competitors, you should be up front about who you are. Your stakeholders deserve nothing less. (By the way, Mackey has resumed blogging but now uses his real name.)

Now look at McDonald's, a great brand that's using the social web to get customer dialogue back on track. Its web sites are becoming very social in nature, especially focused around nutrition, and WiFi access is making its outlets more social, as well. The company has a deal to sell coffee from Newman's Own—a company with a social conscience that MacDonald's hopes will rub off, not a small consideration.

The concept of moral purpose in branding is coming to life in the social web. By moral purpose, I mean offering value and acting ethically and transparently. No business will succeed without a clear definition of its transparency in doing business. The ethics around doing business include: environmental responsibility, diversity in employment, considering the larger effect of the company's actions. In other words, you need to have moral purpose embedded in your values, along with great products at a great price. The real issue is to learn how to market on the social web responsibly. But first, let me talk a little more about what the social web means to marketers.

2

Community and Content: The Marketer's New Job

(Or How to Cut Your Marketing Budget and Reach More People)

Although the next generation of marketing is in its infancy, the social web is already having an effect. More to the point, you're going to be caught up in it, no matter what kind of business you're in. Marketing's goals will remain the same as they've always been—to attract and retain customers. However, marketing's role has changed, and the social web is promoting that change.

"Customers are demanding to be more engaged with the companies that affect their lives," is how Diane Hessan describes the change. As president and CEO of Communispace, which builds and runs private online customer communities, Diane sees unmistakable signs that the social web is part of that change. "Booming trends like blogging, online communities, flash mobbing, buzz agents, and MySpace show that customers have a lot to say—they want to be asked and they want to be involved." If you haven't already heard about flash mobbing and buzz agents, you soon will. Flash mobbing is assembling a group of people via the Internet or other digital communications networks; they suddenly appear in a public place, do something unusual for a brief time, and then disperse. Buzz agents are recruited for the purpose of shilling; they talk up the product or service without identifying their connection to the company.

For a glimpse at the social web's influence on the role of marketing, consider GlaxoSmithKline's experience with Communispace. In preparation for the launch of its first weight reduction product, Glaxo sponsored an online weight loss community. This was a real win-win. The members benefited by meeting other women who supported their dieting struggles through instant messaging and chat discussions. Glaxo benefited as the members answered questions about product packaging, offered advice on where to place the product in stores, and, most significantly, discussed their battles with the scale.

These community discussions helped shape Glaxo's advertising and packaging for the company's diet pill. They also uncovered rampant confusion about dieting. As *BusinessWeek* reported, "In one exchange, a member stated that you could lose weight by drinking eight glasses of water a day, while another said no, it's eight quarts. A third added that the water doesn't count if it's in coffee, but this person was quickly contradicted."

Over time, community members come to trust one another even though they may be scattered all over the country, and their responses can be quite revealing. When Glaxo asked the group to use images that showed how they felt about themselves, the women posted photos of hippos and elephants. Says Andrea Harkins, senior research manager at GlaxoSmithKline Consumer Healthcare: "These are things they wouldn't have said in words."

In the end, the online community gave Glaxo far more information than it could have obtained from focus groups. As an additional benefit, the community has created an intensely enthusiastic corps of product evangelists. One member said about Glaxo, "They have done an incredible job of reaching out into the community and giving us all hope that someone out there cares about us and we are not alone in our struggle to lose weight."[1] The marketer's new job is to build communities of interest and provide content. The reason to do so—as the rest of this book will demonstrate—is to cut the marketing budget and reach more people more effectively.

Who's Really in Control Here?

The goal of marketing has always been and will continue to be building and leveraging relationships between your organization and various customers—current and prospective consumers of your products and services plus employees, partners, shareholders, government, the media, analysts, and all the rest. Obviously, strong relationships are crucial to establishing and extending brand value, strengthening and protecting corporate and product reputation, and boosting demand. But you have to do all this while under constant pressure to improve marketing's return on investment in a highly competitive global economy.

As I suggested in Chapter 1, marketing's traditional tools for getting the word out are growing rusty. Not only are fewer Americans watching broadcast television in both absolute and relative terms, they're avoiding the commercials with the remote, TiVO, or their cable company's DVR. They're avoiding telemarketers through the National Do Not Call Registry, avoiding Internet pop-up, banner, and flash ads through software programs, avoiding radio commercials through the iPod and other digital music devices, and avoiding print ads the way they always did—by turning the page.

As a result, the job of national advertisers is more complicated than ever; it's more work and expense to run ads in several places than it is to deal with one major magazine or three dominant television networks. For smaller advertisers, the changes have meant they can afford targeted vehicles in which to advertise. But for most advertisers, the growth of vehicles has meant that their advertising becomes more efficient—if they can define their target market well, they can probably find a vehicle that reaches that target market. It's the difference between advertising Titleist clubs in *Time* and in *Golf Digest*.

The control of information, however, continues to shift from marketers to consumers. The explosion of media choice has undermined the mass marketing model because it is dramatically harder to put together a mass audience than it was when everyone you wanted to reach was watching just three television networks. Today, the computer and mobile phones allow consumers to find what they want when they want it. You're not in control any more.

If you're marketing a travel-related product or service, for instance, you need to get involved with the mobile space so people on the go can find you when and where they choose. "Mobile is considered to be an arm of quick-access information," points out Bob Walczak, CEO of Ringleader, a mobile publisher and advertiser network. To connect with customers when they're actively searching for information, Walczak says, "hotels, rental car companies, all those kinds of brands should be associated with the mobile environment."

That's why Burger King's web site has a "BK Mobile" page inviting customers to enter "wap.bk.com" on any mobile phone web browser and find the nearest Burger King restaurant. Or if a customer wants to know how many calories are in that Whopper Junior before taking a bite, it's easy to look it up using BK Mobile. The customer is in control.

Consumers love control so much that when they hear about devices like TiVo and DVRs they want them mainly for the control they offer. They can watch a program when they want, not when it conflicts with a child's music lesson or a client meeting. Apple's iPod and its competitors have profited from this attitude. Once people get used to the idea that they can have their news and weather when they want them and how they want them, and they can have their television when they want it and how they want it, they wonder, "Why can't I have my music when I want it—without commercials?"

Forrester Research did a study a while ago that investigated consumer rejection of advertising. The researchers asked about consumers' level of interest in things like digital video recorders and ad-blocking software. They also asked about interest in a device that would record and play radio content while automatically rejecting commercials—basically a TiVo for radio, although no such thing existed. Consumers were just as interested in the nonexistent radio recorder as they were in the television recorder. All they had to do was hear about it—a new way to take control!—and they wanted it.

Consumers now have access to devices to control their choice of entertainment, news, information, and diversions so there's no going back to the days when a deep-pocketed advertiser could buy the same time on all three television networks and set up a roadblock to overcome channel switching. People who want to watch *The Daily Show* or *House* without commercials will have to wait for the DVD. Or, they can download the episode with commercials at hulu.com. PBS is finding that many people are watching *Frontline* online because they can watch whenever it is convenient for them.

Think your company (or any company) has any control over what consumers hear, see, watch, read, or do these days? In my experience, you actually have less control than ever. True, old habits die hard and company personalities change glacially. As consumers are doing their best to avoid commercial messages, some marketers are dreaming up ways to slip past their defenses. Thus, consumers are served up commercials before movie showings; blatant product placement in video games, movies, and television shows like *American Idol*; and commercials on in-store and airport television networks. Even the bathroom is no refuge: consider the "Wizmark," which, sensitive to very slight motion, will light up, play music, and deliver an advertising pitch from within a men's urinal to a briefly captive audience of one.

The techniques du jour are viral marketing, buzz marketing, word-of-mouth/word-of-mouse marketing, or stealth marketing—the idea that a company can hire people to pretend to be consumers to recommend a product or service. A liquor company might hire attractive young women to visit crowded bars, order the advertiser's product, then turn to the next person and say, "This is really delicious; you ought to try one of these."

If you live in Norwalk, Connecticut, you may have heard of Bobby Choice. His web site is filled with videos, photos, and e-mails complaining about a lack of alternatives to the local cable provider, Cablevision. In his quest for choice, Mr. Choice has also run newspaper ads, made the rounds of Norwalk bars, and handed out free T-shirts. If you think Mr. Choice is simply outspoken or possibly disgruntled, think again: he's actually a stealth campaign for AT&T's U-verse TV service.[2]

I think AT&T could have made a better call. These days, its brand and logo do appear on pop-ups and promotions that litter the Bobby Choice site, but the campaign still looks and feels like one man raging against the system. The harm stealth marketing does to a company's reputation when the deception is revealed (which happens sooner than ever on the Web these days) cannot be offset by any short-term gain in sales or publicity. Marketing has to be both honest and transparent; consumers are cynical enough now—and they are hypersensitive to corporate misbehavior.

We've had 200-plus years of supply-side economy and now we are oversupplied. In an oversupplied world, you have to connect consumers to your products and services. To earn loyalty, you have to build and nurture your customer communities.

Marketers therefore have two daunting challenges. First, you have to justify your spending and your budgets through better performance measurement. The pressure is on from senior management to be much more transparent about marketing investments and the return on those investments. Second, you must connect with customers and prospects who are increasingly harder to reach. How do you deliver a message that resonates with customers and induces them to buy what you're selling?

The objective is to have customers invite you to deliver the message to them. You just can't force it on them any more.

Marketing's Role Has Changed

As I've already suggested, the explosive growth of the social web has changed the marketer's role from a *broadcaster* pushing out messages and materials to an *aggregator* who brings together content, enables collaboration, and builds and participates in communities. As an aggregator, you bring together content, collaborate with your customers, and engage your online communities. Content includes new ideas, research, and opinions. Collaboration creates an open environment in which people can, and do, share knowledge. The aggregator extends invitations to individuals as well as to groups to join communities of interest.

Most stories about the social web focus on the "cool" aspects, such as YouTube.com (everyone can be a movie actor/director/producer) or Facebook.com and MySpace.com (talk to friends, meet people, network with coworkers). Despite all the chatter, there is a strong business case for integrating the social web into your marketing toolkit. The social web provides numerous opportunities for strengthening and expanding relationships with all your customers. These opportunities include:

- *Targeted brand building.* Depending on the size and breadth of a company's customer base, communities can be organized by vertical market (e.g., high tech, energy, consumer packaged goods, retail, automotive) or by horizontal topics that cut across multiple sectors (e.g., finance, manufacturing, the environment). To build your organization's brand, consider hosting a podcast—an online audio that users can download to a device such as an iPod—on a hot topic such as change management, outsourcing, risk management, corporate governance, innovation, or talent management. Sessions could be moderated by an analyst or a journalist and feature customers sharing their experiences with their peers. Senior executive blogs and microsites (web sites developed with a particular focus for a specific target audience) can help establish industry thought leadership.

- *Lead generation.* At launch time, you can introduce the new product or service both in the online and offline worlds. Using the Web, you can reach more people—and reach highly targeted markets—more quickly and more cost-effectively than through traditional broadcast and print media. You can stimulate lead generation by, say, offering a white paper in return for having people register on your site and give you some basic information. You can encourage product trials through online demonstrations. You can attract prospective customers to online contests.

- *Partnerships.* In addition to customers and prospects, the social web is a great tool for staying connected with distributors, technology vendors, manufacturers, and other business partners. Often companies announce these partnerships with great fanfare but they fade away over time because it requires a significant effort to maintain them. An e-community or social network can help your company's distributors, store managers, sales representatives, and others stay in touch and consult with one another. A community is a flexible platform for your partners to receive the latest company updates, news from the head office, and stories from the field.

- *Research and development.* Isolation is the greatest obstacle to product and service innovation. Conversely, collaboration stimulates new ideas and new approaches that can lead to breakthrough solutions to complex problems. Blogs, wikis (web sites that allow users to add, remove, or edit content easily), online communities, and social networks can bring product developers together in real time. Procter & Gamble has set up pgconnectdevelop.com to attract new product designs and technologies from outside the organization. Scientists can get immediate feedback on research, make corrections, and move on to the next challenge. Some businesses have built private online communities to obtain consumer input on new products during development. As GlaxoSmithKline learned, by including customers in the product development process, companies can forge bonds that foster long-term product or brand loyalty.

- *Employee communications.* The social web tools also afford numerous opportunities to strengthen and expand employee communications. For example, internal webcasts—using streaming media technology to take a single source such as the CEO, head of marketing, or even the union president and distribute it to many listeners/viewers at one time—can provide employees with updates on specific topics such as new accounting rules or new product features. You can distribute company news or human resource benefits information to mobile devices as a way to stay in touch with employees who travel extensively or spend most of their time at client sites. You can create private online forums where salespeople share experiences and ask each other for advice. If you're looking for new talent, you can tap into business or career networks such as LinkedIn.com or Vault.com to identify and reach prospective employees.

All of these strategies incorporate significant enterprise-generated content. In the social media world, material that traditionally has appeared in published form—ads, press releases, brochures, articles, white papers, and the like—is generated to facilitate participation and interaction. Johnson & Johnson sponsors a network of BabyCenter web sites featuring advice and online forums for parents and parents-to-be. It also hosts microsites for specific products and campaigns, such as touchingbond.com for its Johnson's Baby Lotion. The company posts videos and animated vignettes with advice and how-tos for new parents, such as showing how moms can bond with their babies through massage (using Johnson's Baby Lotion, of course).

The "About BabyCenter" page clearly states that J&J owns the network, reassures visitors that editorial material is fact checked and reviewed by medical authorities, and leaves no uncertainty about transparency: "We believe you should always know the source of the information you're reading. We never allow advertisers to influence editorial content, and all advertising is either clearly separated from editorial content (in standard placements such as banner ads and right-hand units), or clearly labeled "advertisement" or "from our sponsors."[3]

Opportunities to Achieve Community

How can you and your company get involved? You can either join in other people's communities or create your own destinations and invite others to join in the conversation there. Or you can do both.

Depending on your marketing goal, it is possible to join all kinds of conversations both as an organization and as an individual within the organization. The advantage of joining another organization's community, like Facebook or YouTube, is that it already has members who come to it regularly. On the other hand, you may not be able to find the exact community you need, so you have to create your own.

For example, Starbucks started mystarbucksidea.force.com and said flat out, "You know better than anyone else what you want from Starbucks. So tell us. What's your Starbucks Idea? Revolutionary or simple—we want to hear it. Share your ideas, tell us what you think of other people's ideas and join the discussion." Within days the site had received something like 100,000 suggestions; it was basically an online suggestion box or focus group. Then, with the announcement that Starbucks planned to close 600 stores across the nation, some of those customers opened their own communities, trying to save local Starbucks. One community can spawn another once the conversation starts.

In this case, Starbucks did not create a microsite on its existing web site, but bought an off-the-shelf community platform. Salesforce.com offers one, as does Mzinga.com, KickApps.com, Neighborhood America, and others. For many companies, these independent destinations have all the community functionality they need.

Here are other examples of communities that meet different marketing goals:

> Segway established social.segway.com for Segway owners. It allows them to map trails, track mileage, discuss ownership benefits, find other Segway owners in their communities, and more. Owners share information and ask questions about the best way to maintain a Segway. The site is a way to involve owners with the product. You're not just a weirdo riding a two-wheeled vehicle; there are others like you.
>
> H&R Block launched a community called Digits at digits.hrblock.com, which is all about understanding personal income taxes, tax breaks, deductions, and connecting directly with other H&R Block customers. It integrates with the H&R Block Facebook application (which has something like 7,000 members) and a Twitter personality who during the tax season sends tweets

(brief messages) about trends in how people are filing their taxes. The site promotes the idea that H&R Block is *the* authority on personal income taxes.

To engage fans of NBC's show "The Office" the network launched a community around Dunder Mifflin, the fake company in which "The Office" is set (dundermifflininfinity.com). Fans can interact in the online community as if the company existed, setting up "branch offices," competing for "Employee of the Month," and more. Fans who become involved with the site—where they are called "employees"—intensify their engagement with the show.

NASA re-launched its web site (nasa.gov) to include social media tools in an effort to reach 18- to 25-year-olds and encourage them to join the agency. Visitors can easily create profiles to connect with others interested in the space program.

While these four examples suggest effective ways to use the social web, not every product lends itself to it. In an effort to promote the new "Breeze" cat litter, Purina launched a community for customers to chat about their experiences with litter and using the new product. From what we've seen, however, people really don't want to come together and chat about kitty litter; when I checked, it looked as if 14 people had participated.

This is not much beyond Marketing 101. You must know what business result you're trying to achieve, use relevant traditional marketing tactics and strategies that have proven effective, and then get a little help to leverage some of the new tools that are available today.

New Rules of Engagement

Bear in mind that the social media world is very different from a traditional communications environment. In the traditional communications model, your organization controls content creation and distribution. In the social media world, you have little to no control over content or distribution. Individuals communicate with other individuals and with groups, and groups communicate with individuals and groups—everyone with everyone. It's highly democratic: Everyone has access and everyone can participate. As a marketer, you go to other people's "parties" as well as create your own destinations for other people to come to you.

So what happens, for example, when employees start blogging? Are there rules? Is profanity or character defamation (which may appear in some blogs) going to be permitted? How openly can employees discuss product development? What is considered company confidential information and what is open to the public? Organizations need to establish rules that guide people and help them use the social web tools safely and confidently. I'll be talking about rules in the chapter about blogging.

When you think about rules for participating in the social web, you also face larger issues for corporate governance, especially in terms of promoting accountability, fairness, and transparency. How accountable is the organization for what an employee says in a blog? What kinds of comments are "fair" or "unfair"? What does transparency mean when an employee participates in an online community? Is there an obligation to disclose company affiliation? Can employees have a private life on the Web? If you establish clear policies at the outset, you'll save time and aggravation when the inevitable crisis occurs.

How you manage organizational change is affected by the move from traditional communications to the social web environment. Your employees need to understand the new approach and the new rules of engagement. Now is the time to arrange extensive training for managers, bloggers, corporate communicators, human resource professionals, Web strategists, and others who will be engaging in the social web activities. Educate your employees about best practices and provide rewards for applying these practices.

There are also new rules for measuring marketing success in a social web context. The new success measures include share of voice, level of engagement, tone of discourse, evidence/quality of community, and cost of market share. How often is your organization being discussed in the blogosphere? Who's doing the talking and how influential are the participants? What are they saying? Are there recurring themes? Is the tone positive, negative, or neutral? Who's listened to the podcast? Who's downloaded the white paper? Are they asking for more information? How many people participated in the online contest and who are they? What was the impact on leads and sales? Some of these measures are quantifiable and others are qualitative.

Up to a point, the Web itself is inherently measurable, a big plus in this era of marketing accountability. At the very least, you can measure where site visitors are coming from (the referring site), which pages they are clicking through, and where they go next without identifying the visitors themselves. You can learn an extraordinary amount but be aware that the costs can be quite high. Therefore, you have to determine the most important metrics needed to attain the best ROI. I'll talk in more detail about ways to measure the social web later in the book.

Finally, how does the social web fit with your company's digital vision? Digital vision is the long-term strategy for the company's entire online presence. How will you use the web site (or web sites) to support customer relationship management and online service and support—and how will the social web fit into that framework? Social media is not something to bolt onto a web site; it should be an integral part of a company's overall online experience.

You already know that the social web can amplify awareness of your brand, product, or service. Incorporating digital channels into a new product or service launch can help you quickly and cost-effectively reach highly targeted prospects. Communities can serve as referral networks: an opinion leader in the community "endorses" a new product and in a flash other members are downloading the free trial and asking for more information.

In fact, the social web can play a valuable role throughout the entire life cycle of product development, market introduction, and market adoption. During the development phase, you might use blogs, wikis, communities, or all three to get feedback on various product features. During market introduction, you can use podcasts and webinars to engage and educate potential customers about the new product's benefits and applications. (A webinar is a seminar conducted over the web; unlike a webcast, a webinar is designed to be interactive.)

As the product begins to sell, you can use the social web for trouble-shooting, problem solving, and customer service and support—plus the all-important word-of-mouth to build that buzz.

By now, the benefits of marketing to the social web should be apparent—and viewed as essential to an overall marketing strategy. The social web allows you to engage and influence prospects and customers and build trusted relationships over time. It helps you learn what employees, clients, and partners really think about new products, programs, or other initiatives. And all of this is in near real-time and for a fraction of the cost of traditional media. But if you build a site to attract a community, will anyone come?

Making the Transition to the Social Web

(First Change Your Marketing Mindset)

The future is here (but you knew that). Remember how national publications, national radio, and national television led to the rise of mass marketing? That was the first period of marketing. The second period—which is just about over—saw the rise of direct marketing through direct mail, telemarketing, and catalogs.

Now we're in the third period of marketing, the era of the social web. Your customers (and potential customers) are more in control of what they read, hear, and watch. And not only do they want to talk to other people, they want you—the marketer—to listen to them. It's time to embrace this new reality. But how do you make the transition from the old marketing to the new marketing of the social web?

The first thing you have to do is change your marketing mindset (see Table 3.1). Then you'll be in a good position to change your approach to brand equity, segmentation, targeting, communication, content, virality, reviews, the role of advertisers and publishers, the hierarchy of information, and—inevitably—payment.

This is not just another 12-step program. It's a great way to organize your thinking about the differences between the traditional

TABLE 3.1   Old Marketing versus New Marketing

Components	Old Marketing	New Marketing
Marketing mindset	Use one-way, one-sided communication to tell brand story.	Nurture dialogue and relationships; be more transparent, earn trust, build credibility.
Brand equity	Brand recall is holy grail.	Brand value is determined by customers: How likely are customers to highly recommend the good or service?
Segmentation	Group customers by demographics.	Group customers by behavior, attitudes, and interests—what's important to them.
Targeting	Target by demographics, especially for media buying.	Target according to customer behavior.
Communication	Broadcast style: create and push message out for customers to absorb.	Digital environment for interactive communication through search and query, customer comments, personal reviews, or dialogue.
Content	Professional content created and controlled by marketers.	Mix of professional and user-generated content, increasingly visual.

Virality	A nice feature but popularity too often driven by flashy presentation rather than content.	Virality based on solid content about remarkable products or features that will get people talking and forwarding e-mail.
Reviews	Think Michelin Guide: the experts weigh in.	Think Zagat or Amazon: users review and vote on everything.
Advertiser/ Publisher role	Publisher establishes channel and controls content to gather an audience for the advertisers who sponsor channels or programs.	Build relationships by sponsoring (not controlling) content and interaction when, where, and how customers want it.
Strategy	Top-down strategy imposed by senior management drives tactics.	Bottom-up strategy builds on winning ideas culled from constant testing and customer input.
Hierarchy	Information is organized into channels, folders, and categories to suit advertisers.	Information is available on demand by keyword, to suit users.
Payment	Cost per Thousand (CPM): Emphasis on cost; advertisers buy with the idea that share of voice = share of mind = share of market.	Return on Investment (ROI): Invest in marketing for future growth and profitability based on measurable return.

marketing of yesterday and the new marketing of today and tomorrow, starting with a new mindset.

The New Marketing Mindset

As we saw in the last chapter, marketing's role has not changed. It's still about defining target markets, communicating with prospective customers, building loyalty, and so on. But the techniques that were successful in the past will be less and less effective in the future. This is where your new marketing mindset comes in.

Clear your mind of all those one-way, one-sided communication techniques, all those ways of spouting only your side of the story. Marketing to the social web is not about you getting *your* story out; it's about your customers. It's about being more transparent, earning trust, and building credibility. It's about nurturing relationships and dialogue among customers, prospects, your company, and whoever else is active in the community.

To win the branding war, you have to recognize that brand equity is shifting away from brand essence and brand recall. Those were key elements in the old marketing and resulted in what I call the *stationary* brands, like Gillette, Kodak, Disney, and Kellogg's.

But a brand is actually a living, changing thing, especially in the new marketing. It is difficult for many marketing people and C-level executives to admit that their brand is a living thing. Yet, in the new marketing reality, the brand is based on the dialogue you have with your customers and prospects—the stronger the dialogue, the stronger the brand; the weaker the dialogue, the weaker the brand.

What makes the social web so important is that it permits companies to have these kinds of dialogues more efficiently and less expensively than ever in the past. Google is a good example of a living brand that fosters dialogue. Its various products enable dialogue between users in so many ways—features like Google Talk, Google Mobile, Google Groups, Blogger, YouTube, and Picasa. The brand has become iconic because it's an indispensable part of everyday life for anyone who uses a computer (or a cell phone). Google is always developing new features, asking for feedback on "beta" elements, and checking to see what people do with Google.

In the new marketing, companies gauge brand equity not by static measures such as brand recall but by dynamic measures such as customer word-of-mouth. One useful tool is the net promoter score (NPS). A metric developed by loyalty guru Fred Reichheld, the NPS indicates how likely your customers are to recommend your company to friends or colleagues. (See www.netpromoter.com for more.)

To see NPS in action, consider Intuit's experience. Known for QuickBooks, Quicken, TurboTax, and other financial software packages, Intuit uses a series of NPS surveys to uncover what its 20 million customers really think of its products and services. Instead of simply calculating scores and tracking their ups and downs, Intuit digs deeper to learn why customers are or aren't willing to recommend specific products.

TurboTax, for instance, was losing market share when the company undertook NPS surveys and invited thousands of promoters and detractors to suggest high-priority improvements. After Intuit implemented the ideas, which included better technical support and streamlined software installation, TurboTax's NPS scores started to rise—and so did market share. "I tell employees not to focus on the score," explains Intuit founder Scott Cook. "Focus on what improvements you can make in service to improve the score."[1]

Segment by What People Do, Feel, Think

As I said in Chapter 1, companies have traditionally segmented their markets according to easily identifiable demographics like age, gender, education, and income. In the second period of marketing, they added lifestyle factors such as diet or medical concerns. With the advent of the social web, the new marketing means segmenting by what people do and feel—their behavior as well as their attitudes and interests. Your goal is to identify groups of customers within the larger market that you can reach and affect through your marketing.

Segmenting by behavior, attitudes, and interests doesn't depend on faceless numbers (how old customers are or how wealthy they are, for instance). Instead, it groups people by what's important to them, as indicated by what they do, think, like, and dislike. Once you know what moves your customers, you can target them with marketing activities that are meaningful to them. (It's all about them, after all.)

The old way of targeting was by demographics. This has probably been beaten into marketers' heads because it tends to be the way to buy media. Not in the new marketing. Now the Web helps us map behavior (on the Web itself) very closely. Age, sex, educational level, income, and other demographic indicators do not even register online (with the exception of web sites for children or for products like liquor, where age is very important for legal reasons). As the famous *New Yorker* cartoon pointed out, on the Web, nobody knows if you're a dog. Software can track behavior, however, through the sites customers have been visiting, how long they linger on each page, and many other details. This opens the door to precise targeting opportunities.

Suppose a customer begins visiting web sites related to flat panel television sets. One place she might look is on CNET.com. If you are Samsung, you might buy a link on CNET that says, "Special today on Samsung flat panel screens! Click here." The customer doesn't have to deal with the whole Samsung web site but is taken right to a description of a very targeted offer.

Ultimately, the social web will lead to targeting customers who say, "Here are the things I like. Make me an offer, instead of my having to do all the work." Customers will be more open to targeting based on behavior because they've made the choice, they have the control. Marketing is not an irritation or an interruption if it relates to something customers want. The ideal is to get your brand in front of just the people who are interested in your product or service at this time.

This applies to paid media as well; paid media needs to support the growth of social media. For example, Samsung should also be sponsoring forums on what people like about its flat panel television sets or doing consumer comparisons with Panasonic or Sharp sets. It should participate in blogs that talk about flat panel television sets.

One of the big changes happening with the social web is a swing away from one-to-one targeting. I think marketers went too far in that direction, to a point of diminishing returns. We don't need to know every little thing about an individual. We do need to know that an individual participates in three or four online communities of interest on any given day. We might learn, for example, that a customer is interested in a car today because he's visiting a community subgroup about convertibles. Targeting is moving more to groups of interests and behaviors rather than to a narrow one-to-one approach.

Think of what you can do with targeting in the mobile environment, for instance. Bob Walczak, CEO of the mobile publisher and advertising network Ringleader, tells me his company can target audiences in a number of ways. If a company wants to reach sports lovers via mobile, Ringleader can content just that content category. Ringleader can also target behaviorally, according to how the mobile phone subscriber uses the device. Maybe one mobile customer searches the web for information while another does a lot of texting. Understanding how your customers behave (in this case, how they communicate when they're on the go) will help you reach them through the social web.

Communicate Interactively

The new marketing creates the platform of true interactivity. Add more dimensions to the communication, rather than having most of the communication flowing from the organization. So you might add the ability to search and query, which is similar to search; add dialogue; add comments; add personal reviews of products, services, experiences.

Communication is less about creating contained and controlled messages (as in the old marketing) and more about creating compelling environments to which people are attracted. Remember, the marketer's primary job is to be the aggregator of customers and potential customers; from that aggregation a percentage of potential customers will become paying customers. The marketer's secondary job is to create compelling environments that attract the kinds of people who are likely to become paying customers because of the way they think, feel, act, or all three.

How do you create an environment that is a shared, powerful experience? Starbucks is a great example of environmental marketing because it is a physical place where people want to visit and stay a long time. Amazon is a great example of early environmental marketing because people actually hung out at the Amazon web site. They wrote about the books they liked and didn't like and made lists for other visitors. Oracle and IBM are two business-to-business examples of how to create digital environments that are thoughtful, attractive, and foster interactive communication.

Content Created by Customers

In the new marketing, the best web sites will combine professional and user-generated content (contributed by customers and potential customers). You're asking for this—encouraging it—when you create an environment where it's easy to talk about your products or services. Even when you pay for and develop professional content, user-generated content continues the dialogue.

Here's what I mean about balancing professional and customer-generated content. You have every right as, say, a leading energy company to post your thoughts about the future of electricity. Customers will let you know whether they agree or disagree. You can offer podcasts from an expert on energy from the University of California, who talks about the future of renewable energy. Again, customers will react to this professional content with their own content.

Another difference between the old and new marketing is that content is increasingly visual. You see it now with YouTube; you also see it on business-to-business sites like Red Hat, Cisco, and Motorola, which have visual content customers can watch, download, interact with, or all three. It's almost embarrassingly easy to create a video with a video camera, digital camera, cell phone, or computer. Of course, the video may not be very slick, but that is often the point.

Let me point out, at the risk of sounding profound in a clichéd way, that everybody has become media. So as you get into the social web, you are media. Individuals are media, organizations are media.

They are writers, editors, and publishers—sorting, prioritizing, and presenting compelling content in an interesting way that makes it important.

For many years, the huge expense of broadcast journalism was the filming and editing. Today, however, the quality of visuals made on a shoestring is quite amazing. Small to mid-size companies with a video camera and a computer can produce acceptable-quality videos to post on a web site or e-mail to interested customers. Entrepreneurs with expertise are already posting how-to videos on YouTube or specialized sites like ExpertVillage.com, Howcast.com, and Wonderhowto.com to build name recognition and drum up some business.

Viva Virality

Viral marketing is interesting because it's word-of-mouth over which you have no control. Before I go on, a word about silly virals such as the Burger King "Subservient Chicken." At www.subservientchicken.com, a camera reveals a person in a chicken costume standing in a dingy living room. The chicken responds to typed commands, such as "tap dance," "take a bow," or "do push-ups." Within 17 months, the site had been visited more than 422 million times. This popularity set off a chain-reaction of viral ads made to be funny, charming, sexy, or controversial so people would e-mail them to friends or post them on web sites.

My twelve-year-old son thought it was a howl when he found an animated hippopotamus singing a song, and he kept e-mailing it to his friends. So even at a twelve-year-old's level, we can see the effect of virality.

Yet silly virality, for all its popularity, is not really word-of-mouth. The concept we should be talking about is content-based virality. How do companies get solid viral content, something that does more than simply attract attention to itself? In healthcare, the content could be about lowering cholesterol or improving quality of life. People talking to other people about these topics will create a viral dialogue with content.

If you do a viral campaign, make sure the content makes sense for your brand. Millions of people took advantage of Office Max's holiday season campaigns to paste a face on a cute dancing elf and e-mail the link to friends and family (elfyourself.com). Similarly, the retailer S&K Menswear invited visitors to paste Dad's face on a costumed dancing figure for a fun Father's Day e-mail card (dancingdaddy.com). Both have fun content for sharing and an attitude that's right for those brands. Virality can work in a far more controlled and smaller community-based way than having to reach 422 million people to be successful.

Marketers should always be thinking about powerful content that people will want to share and make it really easy to share. A whole new generation of technology companies is working on this very issue. There's ExpoTV, sort of a cross between YouTube and *Consumer Reports*. ExpoTV makes it easy for anyone with a video camera to share ideas, information, and opinions about everything from arts and crafts to video games and players. This field is evolving, but the point is: Be sure your site passes the share test. Stop thinking about the Subservient Chicken and think about more engaging content that will interest smaller groups of customers.

Five Stars for Reviews

In the old marketing, customers turned to professional book, theater, movie, and restaurant reviewers for knowledgeable opinions. Once Zagat and Amazon invited ordinary people to give their opinions, there was no stopping the trend, the "Zagatization" of everything. *Consumer Reports* and the experts will always have their place, but in the new marketing, expect customers to vote on everything from cruise lines to cookware.

Customer reviews become particularly important for things that people don't do very often—such as rafting down the Grand Canyon or buying an ultralight airplane. Reviews include big ticket items, drugs, cosmetics, and many other things that affect the body. They will also be important for local and small businesses to enhance the experience of being part of a family of customers. If you add local search—the ability to find an Indian restaurant in San Diego or a bed-and-breakfast in Asheville—the reviews become exceptionally powerful. You may keep your ad in the Yellow Pages, but why not spend a little time, effort, and money to build your social media site?

In short, don't try to control your customers. The difficulty in the movement toward the social web is the natural instinct of marketers and corporate culture to control the message and the customer. It's difficult to give up control completely, but realize that reviews, as user-generated content, serve to demonstrate your company's transparency.

Advertiser and Publisher Roles: No Paper Needed

We have fewer reasons to kill trees because advertising and publishing for the social web requires no physical objects. Many of us simply throw away the instruction manuals that accompany our products, anyway. In fact, let's put all manuals on the Web. If I threw the manual away when I bought my microwave four years ago, invite me to download another copy from the web site or click to watch a brief video.

The new marketing will be collateral-free, with material that is more compelling, customized, visual, and up-to-date. Information can be a powerful customer relationship tool, but it doesn't have to be printed in an ad or booklet. Customers (and prospects) who want to know how to install a circuit breaker or the right way to paint a house can click to view these kinds of practical videos on Home Depot's web site. This makes it easy to learn before doing a project and then buy online or visit the local Home Depot store for supplies.

Ideally, you want to make content available at the exact moment customers need it. Let people choose what they want to see and when they want to see it, in effect making customers copublishers. The same holds true for advertising. Give up control, give customers real choices (and real content), and their collaboration will make the dialogue more meaningful. You can sponsor a site or community and associate your brand with it, but don't expect to control the dialogue.

Strategy from the Bottom Up

Strategy has traditionally been imposed from the top down. Now it has to be bottom up. As marketers, we have to learn from the people who are really paying attention to our products. Companies should test ideas and products and let the strategy bubble up from there, instead of trickling down from top management. Through the social web you can quickly test, say, 2,000 versions of a new yogurt container and build on the winning version. Suppose you develop a new diet pill. Where should it be displayed in chain drugstores? Where would a prospective customer look for this kind of product? Test that and use the results to drive your strategy.

Clearly, there are other dimensions to strategy. Market leaders must have an overall strategy to stay on top in the automotive industry, soft-drink industry, computer industry. But in a social web world, you have to segment your strategies to the various communities in which you want to participate and sell. If you're an automotive company, how do you communicate to the group that is interested in the environment and energy conservation or the group that cares about speed and sexy looking cars?

Note that the principles here are the same for companies of all sizes, both consumer and business-to-business. Say you manufacture and market shopping carts. How do you communicate with supermarkets, chain drugstores, and other potential customers? Some will be interested in durability, some in looks, some in price. How can you provoke a dialogue so that customers tell you about problems their stores are having with carts or what shoppers are saying about carts?

Hierarchy: Let Users Decide

In the old marketing, information was arranged into channels, folders, and categories to suit advertisers. In other words, the sponsors practically dictated the hierarchy of organization. Not any more. With the social web, information has to be available on demand by keyword, when and how users want it. So when I need to change the cartridge in my ink-jet printer, I have to be able to find that information quickly and easily. Similarly, Samsung should have its information link immediately available to prospects who enter an appropriate keyword ("flat-panel TV").

I'll talk more in later chapters about how information—words, pictures, and sound—on the Web is becoming more and more convenient. The point is that customers want what they want when they want it, and in a way that makes sense to them. This may not necessarily be the hierarchical organization that makes sense to the advertiser or its information technology department.

Companies have traditionally used cost per thousand (CPM) to gauge costs. How much will it cost to reach one million people at prime time in the Boston metro area? How much will it cost for an ad in a magazine with a circulation of 600,000? Notice that CPM puts the focus on the cost that the company must pay.

The new marketing has an entirely different emphasis. Instead of thinking about cost, you'll be thinking about return on investment. Your marketing payment will be based on a measurable return. For example, you might pay according to customer lifetime value (how much a customer is likely to spend with your company during the "life" of your relationship with that customer). In a highly sophisticated situation, the calculation would include the value of that customer's word-of-mouth and referrals.

From this perspective, marketing to the social web is truly an investment in your brand's future growth and profitability. You're paying for that growth, but you have a better idea of what you'll get for your money because the technology allows for more precise monitoring and measurement.

In the new marketing, customers want to be in charge of their own payment options. Whether they use a credit card, give you a bank account number for debit, or choose PayPal, payment options must be fast and easy. From your end, payments via the Web are easy to track and help you analyze where the company's revenue is actually coming from—down to specific customers and offers. That's a big payoff.

Test Driving the Social Web

Now that you know the 12 ways that new marketing differs from old marketing, what can you do to take advantage of these changes? Let's try a thought experiment: What would Ford do if it were planning to market to the social web? What would *I* do if I were suddenly (and improbably) responsible for Ford's marketing?

First, I would want to understand what has worked and what hasn't worked in traditional marketing, so I would begin with an assessment of past efforts. I would then prepare a customer map, paying close attention to the communities I see as the natural Ford communities. These would include current and former Ford owners of every type of vehicle.

Next, I would prioritize Ford's vehicles from the biggest selling vehicle to the slowest seller, not only in absolute terms but in the rate of change from one quarter to the next. Where are sales growing, shrinking? Why have the best-selling vehicles been popular? How have gasoline prices affected vehicle sales? What are the opportunities and threats for each vehicle?

I would look at the Ford dealers, their successes and their dissatisfactions, to see what has worked for them and what hasn't worked. What distinguishes the most effective dealerships from only average dealers? I would look at the manufacturing and how that is tied to product quality and the success of the vehicles. And I would look at the unions—what's good for them, what's bad for them, what Ford can control, and what is out of its control.

As an outsider looking at the corporation, I would tell the top brass that Ford has lost its dialogue with its community. Job number one in the new marketing is to rebuild the dialogue through trust, openness, quality, and all the values that reputable companies hold dear.

After this analysis, I would rebuild digital Ford. I would ensure that the voices of all those communities were heard—and listened to—regularly and seriously. This means hearing what Ford could do better on the cars, what it should get rid of, what models drivers, dealers, and service technicians like or dislike—and why.

Not only would I set up consumer advisory panels, I would set up dealer advisory and service technician panels. Ford should know what policies and procedures the dealers like, what they don't like—and why. These online forums would be password protected and not open to the general public, but used to enable dealers to communicate directly with company executives and with each other.

Although negatives must still be acknowledged and allowed on Ford web sites, I would showcase the value Ford brings to different customers in the form of family vacations, travel tips, fuel efficiency, and saving the planet. These are all issues in which a Ford Motor Company should be involved—moral purpose issues that cut across the customer communities. I would look at energy development and costs; how the population boom will affect the environment when billions of people own (or want to own) cars; the future of the dealership and how can Ford can help its dealers.

Part of marketing to the social web and encouraging a dialogue with customers is also about shaping a future together. In my view, Ford hasn't been shaping the future as much as it has been trying to catch up. In other words, it's been reacting rather than setting a standard like Toyota does—a standard that people admire.

All this would be Phase One of credibility-building and community interest-building and future-shaping. In Phase Two, I would bring some fun back to the brand. Cars are about more than getting people from point A to point B. They've become digital centers, entertainment machines, as you know when you pass a minivan with a color video screen for every child in the back seat. For fun, I would look for some experiential things, perhaps a new and fresh twist on the old Ford Punt, Pass and Kick Contest, which was popular in the 1960s and 1970s.

I would start focusing on the user experience. How can I make Ford into the Apple of automobiles through elegant design and understanding how people actually use their cars? By focusing on the user experience, I would bring in community building, digital communication, partnerships with entertainment companies and content providers, loyalty and discount programs, and even games. I would limit traditional advertising and start experimenting with cutting-edge ideas. Ford could make more use of new media, hold a car design contest for high school students, for instance.

Beyond Bold Moves for Ford

Ford has been easing into social media, bit by bit. One misguided step was its Bold Moves site, created "to present Ford as a company coming to its senses, open to new ideas, and ready to learn from its mistakes." The site included both bad news and good news and invited visitors to post comments and ask questions.

Yet all the videos showed beautiful Ford vehicles near the ocean or crossing a famous bridge—almost purely Ford commercials. I posted a few innocuous comments that never appeared and then posted a horrendous story. Silence. The whole thing seemed manipulative and not terribly transparent. I wasn't surprised when Bold Moves disappeared from the web.

Seth Godin, author of several books on Internet marketing, observes: "Ford doesn't have a PR problem. Ford has a we-were-dependent-on-gas-guzzling-SUVs-until-people-learned-the-truth problem. Ford has a we-don't-reward-great-designers problem. Ford has a dealer problem." Godin says that unless the company gets its cars right, no amount of Internet marketing will help.[2] I say that Ford has to do both, and that an effective dialogue with *all* its customer communities can help it get its cars right. But Bold Moves was not the way to do it.

These days, Ford has moved beyond Bold Moves. Its Owner Services page has a forum link: "A unique gathering place for both owners and enthusiasts, Ford Forum is at the heart of the Ford community." But the link actually took me to an outside site (as Ford warned when I moused over it). I clicked to read posts about future models and getting parts or fixing older Ford models. What I didn't find was the kind of honest give-and-take dialogue that Ford management should be having with its customers and stakeholders.

The Owner Services page also had links to six blogs—and all were on third-party sites. Have a question? The Customer Support page invites questions (110 character limit) that its "automated agent" will answer. No dialogue there. Then I clicked to the "Ford. Drive One" page and watched a couple of Ford videos on crash dummies in action and our hydrogen fuel cell future. Nothing from consumers. I noticed an "Internet buzz" headline but it only linked to reviews on Yahoo! Autos. Sorry, Ford, this is *not* the way to build trust and market to the social web.

I can understand the reluctance of Ford's management to open itself up to the slings and arrows of outrageous fortune, so in the next chapter I'll talk about some of the real problems of the social web.

How to Let Customers Say What they Really Think

(And Keep Your Job)

Should you let customers say whatever they want on your web site? You (and, truth be told, your boss) might instinctively recoil from this idea. And that's understandable, considering all the negative comments floating around the Internet.

Just a five-minute search will show you the depth and breadth of customer dissatisfaction with American business practices. Here, for example, is a rant against Ford posted on complaints.com a couple of months ago (this is a quote, typos and all): "We own a 2006 Volvo XC90, while it's a decent vehicle, it's way overpriced, it gets 14 MPG, and we have had numerous issues with it. The dealer has been great, but i wouldn't reccomend this vehicle to anyone. My real complaint is that we wanted to trade it in, we wanted to buy an american car, specifically a Ford Hybrid. The problem is that they don't have any available, won't have any until Sept of this year at best, and trying to contact Ford for some better answers or results.....their response is that I should call their PR department ???? For some reason they can't forward my emails to their own people? We want to do our part, buy american, and now I see why our American car companies are in trouble, they can't figure out a way to produce the right kind of vehicle, and worse how to create a good customer service channel."[1]

And here's a quote from "1Betty" (screen name) complaining on the my3cents.com site about Avis: "I rented a car in Salt Lake City Utah. Everything was fine. When I returned the vehicle I got out of the car for a couple minutes to find out something in airport. I came out & the officer left a citation with no amount on it. I turned car in and accidentally left cell phone in console. I called back before the plane left which was within an hour and they rented it already and after calling for 4 days they said they didn't find it. I forgot about citation. I rented another car almost 5 months later and find after I turned it in on my account they charged $240 for the citation which was ridiculous. I'm sure the citation & Avis have a deal made. Why did it take them so long to do this. They probably don't put a charge on citation so they can charge whatever. The officer made it seem like it was not a big deal."

I could go on and on, but you get the idea. So back to that thorny question: Should you let people post their comments (the good, the bad, the ugly) on *your* web site?

Learning to Let Go

When I suggest that companies allow ordinary people to comment on—even criticize—their products, services, or store security policies as part of marketing to the social web, the reaction is something like: "Gee, I don't know if we can do that. What am I going to tell my boss?"

The simple answer is: Tell your boss that people are going to criticize anyway, and you're probably better off in the long run letting them do it in your store (or on your site) than in the public square.

The question actually has a number of parts. What are the disadvantages and advantages of allowing public comments on your site? What are the legal issues—libel, plagiarism, defamation? How can the organization be both open and protect itself?

In this first phase of the social web, I believe web sites, microsites, webinars, and communities should be a combination of professional content and customer-generated content. But as a first tentative step into this ocean, you might limit the site to only those tools over which you have total control. You don't have to open your site up to anyone; you can have the professional content developed by experts within your company. All companies, even small businesses, have various subject-matter experts on staff. Let your experts express their opinions and thoughts on the site, which they can do without giving away the store. What they say is content your organization can control.

Hewlett Packard, for instance, posts employee-made videos about technical subjects like digital camera features and not-so-technical subjects like how easy it is to recycle inkjet cartridges. Its more formal corporate videos showcase internal experts talking on topics such as the future of enterprise computing, the best way to store back-up data, and the latest graphics applications for movie animation.

You can also offer content from selected experts. For example, Kodak posts podcasts featuring professional photographers offering tips and tricks for great photos. Although this is content over which your company has less than total control, presumably the outsiders will not attack their hosts any more than a freelance newspaper columnist will attack the paper.

To ease into customer-generated content, I suggest that companies set up at least one place as a forum where customers and anyone who is interested can talk about your products and your company. Start with one product—maybe a product that's a great product you can make better. Don't put out your worst dogs first to be kicked around. In the beginning, at least, you can try to direct the conversation toward your strengths. Then, as you slowly develop trust over time—both with customers/prospects and with senior management—you can open the site to other, more sensitive, topics.

Most of the comment software you might use to screen public comment allows you to choose which comments you want to leave out. In the simplest form, such software acts like a spam filter (you probably know how this works because you have one on your computer). But in addition, there are programs that flag obscene or sensitive words: "sucks," "rip-off," "incompetent," "low quality," and whatever words are touchy in your situation. Someone will have to actually read the flagged posts and decide which should be used.

Inevitably, every organization will receive negative comments, from the fairly benign to "My grandmother was killed when her Pinto was rear-ended." Fortunately, just because you invite public comment, you do not have to publicize every comment. John Palfrey, the director of the Berkman Center for Internet & Society at Harvard Law School, recommends a relatively flexible policy on posting. "If something is unrelated or is spam or both, you delete it," he tells me. "And if somebody says something critical of your product, I think you need to be able and willing to rebut the criticism. Take it head-on."

One of the lessons learned in protecting or promoting a brand online, John says, is that it rarely makes sense to ignore your critics, adding, "By virtue of offering a space to comment on your company, you are inviting those critics right up to your front door. You have to be prepared for them whether you're letting them on your site or you're just reacting to what somebody else blogs elsewhere."

Learning to Listen

Critical information about a company and its products has a way of slipping out anyway. For example, *Automotive News* reported that Mazda dealers Randy Hiley and Robert DeVaux made what they thought was a routine video webcast after the Mazda National Dealer Advisory Council meetings. In it, they mentioned that customer complaints about the RX-8 sports car—squeaky brakes and engine flooding—were unfairly lowering customer-satisfaction scores. Hiley and DeVaux told dealers: "Mazda is well aware of the negative impact on the scores caused by the RX-8 surveys. They agreed with us that the situation had to be changed. And so, effective July 1st, RX-8 will continue to be included in the survey, but the scores will no longer be included in the results."

Someone copied the video and posted it on a Mazda RX-8 enthusiast web site (rx8club.com). From there, the story spread to autoblog.com, an auto enthusiast site. Some unhappy RX-8 owners took the dealers' private webcast comments as evidence that Mazda and the dealers were unwilling to repair their cars swiftly and thoroughly. Autoblog.com noted: "Why would RX-8 owners be surveyed if those survey results were not a factor for the dealer in the end? And more importantly, what incentive would dealers have to give RX-8 owners good customer service if these surveys weren't being counted?"

Here's what Mazda spokesman Jeremy Barnes wrote to members of the Mazda RX-8 forum: "That video is only one portion of the story behind our survey. Mazda's goal is to ensure that our dealers provide all customers, regardless of the vehicle they own, with the highest level of service and customer satisfaction. To assume, after viewing a video posted on the Internet, that Mazda would do anything to compromise this is simply and unequivocally wrong."

Now the carmaker and its dealer council are looking at new ways to communicate with dealers. Said Hiley: "With technology the way it is, it doesn't matter if it's video or e-mail correspondence. Obviously, somebody can get that information somehow. What it tells you is we have to find another medium to communicate with our dealer body that has some security to it."

Ironically, after the webcast circulated, J.D. Power and Associates issued customer-satisfaction scores showing that the RX-8 was Mazda's highest-scoring model. "Those people love their cars," said Robert DeVaux. "The few dealers who sort of put this on the table may have been overreacting."[2]

Fast-forward two years. Mazda decides to extend the RX-8 engine warranty to 8 years or 100,000 miles. Weeks before car owners get the official word, a member of the RX-8 Club site posts a copy of a letter telling dealers about the extended warranty. Next, the site administrator writes that Mazda's Jeremy Barnes has been reading the club's comments and forwarding some to company management. Barnes gives the site an early copy of the company's press release and invites questions from club members after the news becomes public. In other words, Mazda has learned to listen—and to respond.[3]

Comments as Early Warning Signs

Although it took a little time, Mazda's management has come around to the idea that online comments are early warning signs of possible trouble ahead. Dell's struggle with reading the tea leaves of early warning signs was even more public.

When Dell refused to fix or replace his broken computer, Jeff Jarvis, the creator of *Entertainment Weekly*, began posting "Dell Hell" comments on his blog, BuzzMachine. When he had no reaction after several days, he posted an open letter to founder Michael Dell and to Dell's Chief Marketing Officer in which he outlined his struggles with customer service. It struck a nerve with the public. While BuzzMachine frequently receives more than 5,000 visitors per day, Jarvis's "open letter" became the third most linked-to post on the blogosphere one day after it was posted. Traffic on BuzzMachine skyrocketed to more than 10,000 visitors a day (according to Intelliseek's BlogPulse) as other people commented about their bad experiences with Dell customer service.[4]

"What is the NPV [net present value] of Jeff Jarvis' complaint?" asked Pete Blackshaw, the chief marketing officer of Nielsen BuzzMetrics, on his blog. As cofounder of the 2004 Word-of-Mouth Marketing Association, Pete has more than casual interest in this subject. "It's not only the lifetime revenue or 'buyer power' he brings to Dell (probably $15K of buying Dell products over a 15–20 year period), but more importantly, the 'viral power' of his referral network or circle of influence (easily over $200K . . . probably way more)," he wrote.

Call centers and consumer relations departments tend to look at consumers in a vacuum, said Pete; they don't consider customers' circles of influence. "Rarely will you find a web site feedback form that asks consumers whether they blog, spend time on message boards, or share their recommendations with others. Ad agencies and CMOs wax poetic about the importance of profiling, but this thinking rarely seeps over into 'consumer affairs.' We need to reframe our mindset to think about all customer interactions, especially feedback, as an 'advertising' opportunity. If Jeff Jarvis is satisfied with a product, and bothers to speak out, we should have models to estimate the incremental consumer-generated media (CGM) he might generate on behalf of the brand. If he's pissed or frustrated or deeply dissatisfied, our CRM systems should be able to predict with reasonable levels of confidence how much trouble or negative CGM he might stir up. Moreover, this should be a calculus we apply to all consumers, not just the big fish like Jarvis. That said, no one can say Jarvis didn't catalyze a critically important conversation."[5]

There's more. The Jarvis/Dell cause célèbre was high-profile enough that it sparked a white paper, "Measuring the influence of bloggers on corporate reputation," by Market Sentinel (an online monitoring service), Onalytica (a U.K. stakeholder analysis firm), and Immediate Future Ltd (a U.K. public relations agency). The paper concluded, "Jeff Jarvis's BuzzMachine is the key online source for those who have a negative perception of Dell's customer service; its influence is enhanced by support from a closely allied group of bloggers; Dell's own influence on the topic of its poor customer service is weak; Jeff Jarvis's BuzzMachine is the key source for low-influence stakeholders (normally bloggers) writing about Dell customer services in general; taken all in all, Jeff Jarvis's BuzzMachine is the eleventh most influential voice on Dell's customer services in general; if the bloggers were aggregated they would be the second most powerful influence on perceptions of Dell's customer services after Dell itself."[6]

Dell got the message. It quickly beefed up customer service, set up Ideastorm.com to solicit product ideas from customers, and encouraged employees and execs to blog about technology and other topics. Jarvis's Dell Hell was resolved so satisfactorily that he wrote a story about it for *Business Week* and has posted numerous positive comments on BuzzMachine. In short, Dell has steadily been rebuilding trust by encouraging dialogue with its customers.

Thinking about the Dell Hell situation, I suspect there were a couple issues involved here. First, it's sometimes difficult to isolate the truly important complaints from all the "noise." It's akin to the situation you face every working day: Which of all the problems demanding my attention today must be addressed before they become crises? Second, if a particular product happens to have an exceptionally high number of defects, this may overwhelm a system designed for fewer faults. Nevertheless, the Web means that anyone with a grievance can publish it so all the world can read about it (and I mean this literally).

Complaints, Complaints

If you don't start having a dialogue with customers on your site, they will attack your company anyway. As the bloggers become more and more influential (and as it becomes easier and easier for a casual visitor to find relevant blogs through better search tools), a company that has not engaged its customers in dialogue will be at a disadvantage. It would be like ignoring reporters' calls from the *New York Times* or the *Wall Street Journal*. In fact, ignoring negative comments is the equivalent of "No comment," which is the biggest communications mistake executives make. The advantages that come from having openness—which leads to trust, confidence, and respect—outweigh the disadvantages—which lead to suspicion, fear, and contempt.

I'm amazed at how many companies are unaware of the conversations about them already happening on the social web. Senior executives are often shocked that people are talking about everything from safety to design in automobiles, and from efficacy to side effects in drugs. These are deep and broad conversations yet much of the corporate world doesn't know they exist.

Try this: Type "complaints" and the name of your company into a Web browser, and see what's being said about you and your products. While the complaint sites seem to accept almost anything and some of the complaints (like the ones I quoted at the beginning of this chapter) are off the wall, you may find issues to investigate further. Soon the complaint sites are going to be like traditional media; there are going to be wacky ones, but some will rise to the top and become as influential as *Consumer Reports*.

Trust is another major reason to allow critical comments on your site. Andrea, a twenty-something urbanite, tells me she has bought several items from Overstock.com. The site, like Amazon, Netflix, Circuit

City, and others, allows customer comment and although Andrea has posted some mildly unfavorable remarks, they never appeared. She suspects Overstock.com is screening comments and not posting the disapproving ones. As a result, she says, "I don't trust *any* of the comments on the site." Trust once lost is almost impossible to regain.

On the other hand, Amazon.com has permitted critical reviews on its site since 1997, although it offers guidelines and says it will not post reviews that do not follow the rules, which are things like "focus on the book's content," "don't reveal crucial plot elements . . . profanity, obscenities, or spiteful remarks . . . phone numbers, mail addresses, URLs . . ." and the like. Nevertheless, within Amazon.com there are some scathing reviews: "The quality of this book is truly subpar. There are virtually no areas of the book that stand out. It is a poorly structured, hashed-together book with little insight. There is a lot of fluff."

Get used to it: You're going to have complaints and you need to become part of the conversation. Timbuk2 Designs, which makes briefcases and bags, pays close attention to complaints posted on sites like GetSatisfaction.com. "There were a lot of conversations going on outside of Timbuk2, on student blogs and other sites," says Timbuk2's director for marketing, Patti Roll. "Get Satisfaction is a way for us to aggregate that into a format that's easy to utilize." One time, a customer posted a Get Satisfaction complaint saying that Timbuk2 refused to let him cancel an order for a customized bag. Why? The company had already made the bag. Before Timbuk2 could respond, Roll says someone else posted a comment. "They said, 'You're complaining that the service was so fast that they made your custom bag so quickly?' It's exactly what we were hoping to see—customers communicating with customers." Timbuk2 refunded the customer's money and donated the bag to charity, by the way.[7]

What about Legal Issues?

Having your dirty laundry aired in public is one thing, but exposing the company to legal liability is an even bigger worry. Senior executives should consider the legal issues involved in opening a site to public comment, issues such as libel, defamation, and plagiarism. It's natural to worry that the company may be exposed to a lawsuit because of what a customer posts on the web site. For example, what if an anonymous writer claims on your site that one of your dealers stole a customer's down payment? What if a writer claims to have found a severed finger in a bowl of your company's chili?

I'm not going to spend a lot of time on the law here, for two reasons: (1) I'm not a lawyer; and (2) even if I were, these are issues for a lawyer who knows your state's laws. For a good all-purpose introduction to the law in this area, check out the Electronic Frontier Foundation's "Legal Guide for Bloggers" (www.eff.org/bloggers/lg/) and its comparable legal guide to podcasting (http://wiki.creativecommons.org/Welcome_To_The_Podcasting_Legal_Guide).

That said, in general, a libel is any statement that falsely charges any person with crime, or says falsely that someone has been indicted, convicted, or punished for crime; imputes in someone the presence of an infectious, contagious, or loathsome disease; imputes impotence or a want of chastity; or "tends directly to injure someone in respect to his office, profession, trade or business, either by imputing general disqualification in those respects that the office or other occupation peculiarly requires, or by imputing something with reference to his office, profession, trade, or business that has a natural tendency to lessen its profits." Trade libel is defamation against a company or business's goods or services. (The finger in the chili is a trade libel.)[8]

Obviously, if the company libels someone in response to a complaint, that's a problem. But what if a customer, writing on your site, libels someone else—a dealer, a salesperson, a competitor—or plagiarizes copyrighted material? Again, I'm no lawyer, but I think you'll probably be protected under Section 230 of Title 47 of the U.S. Code, which was passed as part of the Communication Decency Act of 1996. Section 230 says, "No provider or user of an interactive computer service shall be treated as the publisher or speaker of any information provided by another information content provider," as federal law, it preempts any state laws to the contrary.

In practical terms, the Electronic Frontier Foundation says that customer comments, "entries written by guest bloggers, tips sent by email, and information provided to you through an RSS feed would all likely be considered information provided by another content provider. This would mean that you would not be held liable for defamatory statements contained in it." The foundation also points to evolving case law: "However, if you selected the third-party information yourself, no court has ruled whether this information would be considered 'provided' to you. One court has limited Section 230 immunity to situations in which the originator 'furnished it to the provider or user under circumstances in which a reasonable person . . . would conclude that the information was provided for publication on the Internet.' "

John Palfrey tells me that while the legal situation is not 100 percent clear, "it is relatively clear that those who host an online service have a safe harbor under Section 230 that indemnifies for most things—people who provide space for other people to post something. My guess is that most companies would be able to avail themselves as a safe harbor site. I don't think it's a big concern."

Be aware that new legal and regulatory guidelines may be on the way, sooner rather than later. For instance, a recent U.K. law cracks down on "bloggers who work secretly to promote companies, brands that pose as consumers on fake blogs and people who [post] false testimonies and reviews on rating web sites such as TripAdvisor or Amazon," writes Mark Sweney in *The Guardian*. The point is that people in the U.K. who are paid to blog about a company or product must now disclose that relationship or face legal action.[9]

To sum up, I understand your boss's reluctance to let customers say what they really think on your site. At the same time, I'm convinced that the benefits outweigh the dangers. You don't have to allow anybody to say anything, any more than you have to accept every spam message that shows up in your mailbox. Still, you're better off allowing your honest critics to have their say because it gives you an opportunity to either explain why they are mistaken or to correct what they've discovered.

You might as well allow customer comments because, again, people are going criticize you anyway, as Dell, Timbuk2, McDonald's, Genzyme, Amway, Starbucks, and other companies have found. As

John Palfrey notes, "There is a sliding scale between constructive feedback and aggressive, destructive behavior. Absolutely, there are people whose online comments will be highly negative, aggressive, and destructive to a company's brands. It's a very real and very difficult problem." In my view, this should not prevent you from soliciting *constructive* feedback.

I have no problem with nice company videos and executive-bylined blogs that tout new products. However, the company needs to be clear that such content is like the special advertising sections in magazines and newspapers, the so-called advertorials. Freelance journalists often write the copy, but it is still a special advertising section, because companies are paying to be included in the coverage. When such material is clearly labeled, I have no problem with it.

I do have a problem with material that is digitally trying to masquerade as real editorial, real social media, real transparentiness (which has the same relationship to transparency that truth has to truthiness). It's fine to have slick, professionally produced video . . . as long as people know you produced it. My favorite comment in a *Forbes* article about the site was that the advertising people are calling what they have done "brand journalism."[10]

If there are journalists who buy that, I would be astonished. If that's the evolution of marketing, count me out. Let me be clear: I respect paid media. Paid media in the new marketing world of the social web will have a huge role, but is still working itself out with banners, buttons, click-throughs, video, brought-to-you bys, downloaded pages, live commercials for live events, and more.

If I were running Ford's marketing, I would create a site called makingFordbetter and invite public comments and discussions in as transparent a way as the First Amendment permits. I'd actually show how customer comments are incorporated into Ford's vehicles. Yes, I'd have less control, but I'd be sparking more conversations and—I hope—building more trust in the Ford organization and in our vehicles.

Seven Steps to Build Your Own Customer Community

Step One: Observe and Create a Customer Map

(Otherwise, You Can't Get There from Here)

Marketing to the social web is increasingly important, but is it right for you and your customers? To avoid the "build it and they will come" syndrome, you have to do your homework, build a solid foundation for your community, and get a dialogue going. So Part II of this book is all about the seven steps and four platforms you need to harness the power of marketing to the social web.

First I'm going to outline the seven steps and then explore each step in more detail, chapter by chapter. To show you how the process works, I'll use Saturn as an example. Let's assume Saturn has four large competitors fighting for the top spot among its particular target consumers: Toyota, Hyundai, BMW Mini Cooper, and Honda. The competitors have been gaining share and consumers no longer value Saturn as a groundbreaking leader in automotive manufacturing and business practices. Management wants to reestablish Saturn's position as the leader of this industry.

If Saturn were a client (it is not) and if Saturn management wanted to market to the social web (and I have no idea what Saturn's management is up to these days), we would first observe what is happening on the Web as it relates to Saturn. That takes us into step 1.

Steps to Marketing on the Social Web

1. *Observe.* Go into the social media and the blogosphere to understand the most influential places within the social web. What are the largest communities? What are they talking about? What is the relevant content? For Saturn, we would search throughout the blogosphere to track conversations from bloggers, analysts, automotive writers, and consumers. What are they saying about the company, its products, and its key competitors? Which automotive brands are generating more buzz and which are the focus of the conversations in the digital world?

2. *Recruit.* To shape a community, you must enlist a core group of people who want to talk about your company, your products, things you are doing, where you are going. This second step is based on the research collected in the first step—you have to know who your recruitment efforts should target.

3. *Evaluate platforms.* What are the best platforms for your marketing goals? Blogs? Reputation aggregators? An e-community? A social network? (Each of these is worth its own chapter.) Some combination of these, or all four? What kind of search tools? Is your audience more interested in listening to things than reading? Are they interested in seeing a lot of things? Do they want to have questions and answers all the time? Do they want to edit? To comment and contribute?

4. *Engage*. Engagement is all about content. How do you build relevant content that will get people coming, talking, responding? How do you build the mix of professional user-generated and enterprise-generated content to do that? Here's where you really get the dialogue going.

5. *Measure*. This is self-explanatory, although somewhat more difficult to do than it might seem at first glance. What do you need to measure? What is your community really connecting with? What are the most relevant metrics?

6. *Promote*. While some sites do not need much promotion (think YouTube or Flickr), most do. You have to get out to the other communities. You have to use the social media to get people talking so they will come back and download things. You have to advertise just as if nothing had changed.

7. *Improve*. Make it better. Add improvements to the site; make it more convenient, more useful, more friendly, more rewarding, more fun.

Now back to our Saturn example. In the "observe" step, after searching Saturn's name, the names of its cars, and its services (e.g., the cars can come installed with the GM OnStar system), we would search for key influencers in the vertical automotive web sites, those that specialize in news and information about cars. One way to find these influencers is based on keyword searches. Another is to use search tools, such as Technorati, Google Blog Search, and others, to narrow the focus. Saturn might suggest keywords such as "automotive services," "top automotive marketing," and "peace-of-mind driving."

From this observation step we might learn that Saturn is not dominating the digital channels. Other automotive companies may be generating more buzz from their online campaigns. We might learn that drivers in Saturn's target market are embracing online tools that make it easier for prospective customers to find information. With these insights, Saturn's management now has a direction and a goal to begin planning the next steps.

Let's dig deeper into how you can take the first step and observe.

Look Who's Talking

During the observation phase, you want to find out what—if anything—people are saying about you on the Web. Are you being talked about in these new channels and platforms in the digital world? Are any blogs covering you? Are any blogs saying anything about your cars? (If you're General Motors and Saturn, obviously they are. In fact, they're talking about your cars—and shoes and ships and sealing wax—even if you are as obscure as Stanguillini Motors.)

Observation helps you get a handle on the landscape. You'll discover what is being said and the conversations that are going on about your company, your products, your category, your competitors, your enthusiasts, your detractors, your suppliers, your partners. These are the groups most important to the fabric of your business.

Who's talking is as important as what they're saying. You need to figure out who is more influential in what is being said. Although 9,000 blogs may have mentioned your car, there may be only 10 that are critical to your reputation, that are growing, and that are becoming as authoritative as *Motor Trend* or the *New York Times*. If you find that autoblog.com is one of those giants, check out what that site's bloggers are saying about Saturn cars.

All of this applies not only to large corporations, but also to fairly small or medium-size companies. Remember, the digital world is a big place with a lot going on. You're likely to find conversations that discuss what you make, what you do, who you compete with, what your customers are saying and buying. No matter what your size, there are digital conversations about you, your industry, and where it is going. (If there actually are no conversations, you have an invaluable opportunity to start one.)

In addition, you have to analyze the influence of new media. This is similar to the media kit that newspapers and magazines have always produced. For instance, check how each medium matches the demographics of your audience: how much money your customers make, where they live, what they eat.

You Need a Business Goal

Within this first step of marketing to the social web, there are a number of research guides that a company should establish before proceeding:

- Identify and prioritize the company's needs and goals.
- Important dates that will determine when in-market activities will need to start.
- Target audience definitions—whom are we most interested in getting a point of view from?
- Products/services to be searched.
- Which languages to search.
- Top four or five competitors.
- Best practice comparisons. Which competitors within the industry or in other industries are using the digital channels to their advantage, particularly social media?
- Keywords for searching the Web.
- Tools audit. Which tools (if any) are we already using to monitor, track, and report?

It should be obvious—but it is not always—that before you begin to think about marketing to the social web, you must have a business goal or marketing goal of some kind. Is there a target market you want to reach more effectively? Do you want to reach a certain market more often? Do you want to change the message for a particular market? You might set a marketing goal around an event such as a product launch. Or you might be experiencing—or think you are about to experience—a crisis of some kind: a product recall, a government investigation, or a strike.

Start by defining the business goal you are trying to achieve through this whole activity and come up with important dates. For instance, if the business goal is a successful product launch of a new product, nail down the date that product is launching and whether there is any kind of prelaunch beta period or anything that might affect the launch.

Define the Target Audience and Speak Their Language

Then you need to define the target audience. Whose point of view is most important to your business? What customer group is your most immediate focus? Do you care about teenagers? Do you care about Java developers? People with diabetes? Quilters? Big 10 football fans? You can define the target audience by behavior, demographics, topical interests, or whatever is relevant to the business goal.

This is an absolutely critical point. As in other marketing efforts, the more precisely you can define your target audience, the more effective your marketing will be. You may discover, for example, that the behavior you are looking for is among people who don't use the Internet much. I have assumed up to this point that the target audience you are trying to listen to and later influence is in fact on the Internet. That may not be true, and once you learn your target is not on the Web, you may want to review your business goals.

You also need to define which products or services are relevant to the business goals. With a new refrigerator, as an example, are you going to look at energy efficiency, recycling issues, service experience, dealer comments, cleaning tips, or some other aspect? With a new sandwich shop, are you going to consider nutrition (a must), variety, breads, condiments, beverages, music, in-store ambience, take-out service, environmental impact? What do people care about? And if you find an issue that the target market seems indifferent toward—such as environmental impact—should you care anyway and take it into account?

You have to decide what languages you are going to search. While English is on its way to becoming the universal language, if you're a global company doing business in Japan, China, South Korea, France, Germany, Spain, or any country where the Internet is significant and English is not, you need to search in the native language. At the end of 2007, the Japanese were the most enthusiastic bloggers in the world; nearly 10 percent of the population had a blog.[1] You should figure out what languages are relevant and have someone with the appropriate skills conduct observation.

Look for Best Practice Examples

Given your business goal and target market, you want to look at competitive web sites (or the subdomains of the web sites) with an eye toward identifying best practices in managing digital conversations. Carefully examine the features and functions and the uses of social media on your competitors' web sites and relevant subdomains. Ideally, you should select one or two sites outside of your direct competitive set that can serve as best-practice examples of specific elements.

For example, Oracle did a flash piece called, "Who Caught John Blade?" and then a followup on a fraud theme, "Who Stole Mark Drake?" (I found both on the Oracle.com site and they may still be available if you search.) The John Blade piece was probably made from a high-end video that was originally produced for major account sales calls. Essentially, it's a who-done-it mystery that takes viewers through a case example of a close call with a terrorist bomber trying to get into a nuclear power facility with a vanload of dynamite. The movie follows characters from the local Georgia police department, Homeland Security, and the Savannah River Nuclear Power facility as they work on their computers, send information back and forth, and try to connect the dots, starting with the theft of dynamite from a construction site all the way to the arrest of the alleged terrorist.

At the end of each snippet of the story, an Oracle spokesperson explains the different Oracle tools used by the characters to swiftly narrow down what is going on and eventually catch John Blade before anything happens. When I first saw it, I thought it was an awesome use of social media. "John Blade" is very interactive, it tells a story, which is always a great way to capture attention in marketing activities, and it's a cool story. "Mark Drake" is also engrossing; both are excellent examples of communicating compelling product information in the digital world.

Another example of how to use social media is IKEA's site (Ikea.com). Click the "Ask Anna" button to bring up an avatar, a graphic representation of an IKEA customer representative that is animated by computer technology. Her text message says, "Welcome to IKEA. I'm Anna, IKEA USA's Automated Online Assistant. You can ask me about IKEA and our products and our services. How can I help you today?" If you type, "I want to redo my bedroom," Anna takes you immediately to the "Beds and Bedding" pages of the site. Given the number of items for sale on the IKEA site, this is an utterly painless and simple way to search for what you want.

Avatars are fairly common now, and studies have found that using an avatar sales agent leads to more satisfaction with the retailer, a more positive attitude toward the product, and greater purchase intention. It is another cut on search functionality and another way to avoid calling the retailer and going through 47 menus in the automated phone system. In principle, the avatar gets customers to their destination faster than clicking or calling and it may help reduce customer calls, which reduces the retailer's costs.

Select Key Words and Begin to Search

Next you want to select 10 to 15 key words, the search terms that lead you to the blogs, the news sites, and the communities that are discussing, mentioning, or rating the topics that concern you most.

Now you're ready to embark on your search. You can use a number of tools here. "Snorkeling tools" (like Cymphony, Nielsen's BuzzMetrics, and Nielsen's Brand Pulse) can identify where you're being mentioned. Search tools (like EveryZing) can help you check for mentions in video, podcasts, and audio files.

But before you begin, find out if somebody within your company is already auditing online conversations. Quite often when we go into a company and propose we do this work, we find that somebody is already using a snorkeling or search tool. Does somebody in your corporate communications, your interactive group, or your Web group (or whatever it's called in your company) have or license any proprietary tools? If so, use them.

All the Internet tools that exist for searching have their strengths and drawbacks. The Web is a Wild West in terms of these tools. But there's a counterintuitive aspect to this: You might assume that because something is on the Web, you'll be able to find and measure it in a very detailed way. Unfortunately, that's not quite true. You have to understand what and how the tool is measuring. And you have to understand and relate what the tool measures to what you're trying to discover.

For example, a free tool called Alexa can search URLs. Type a URL into the Alexa search function and it will tell you the traffic ranking by week, by month, average page views, and more about the way Alexa measures traffic. Here's the catch: Unless the material you are searching incorporates the Alexa tag into its own code, Alexa doesn't pick it up. So the Alexa ranking is only meaningful within the Alexa sphere.

But even if your company has licensed a proprietary tool like Cymphony, you should probably start with what we call the "reputation aggregators," any search capability-type site where the results are automatically ranked: Google, Yahoo!, MSN, Ask, and others.

Now comes the grunt work for which there is no shortcut, no silver bullet. You must search one site after another, using the parameters you have defined and working hard to stick to them (because it is embarrassingly easy to get sucked down rabbit holes). This absolutely requires a pair of intelligent eyeballs connected to the brain of someone who begins to learn the players in the blogs, in the communities, and on the news sites. This person also has to get to know the issues and the lingo at least as thoroughly as somebody who works in the domain. In time, someone with this ability begins to recognize the rhythm of the conversations that are going on and can identify the hot topics and the trends.

This part of the process is difficult to describe exactly. There is no replacement for simply doing it. Use several different Web searching and tracking tools, an extensive database of key influencers and the conversations they have about the product and service, then look for patterns in the key words generated. If you have well-defined parameters, in three to five weeks of reading blogs, forums, postings, and community sites, you should have your finger on the pulse of what is going on.

For example, assume your business goal is a new product introduction. How do you connect your observation to this goal? Think about your best prospects for this new product: What are the characteristics of those prospects? What are the types of things they will want to know? What will interest them in your product?

Now look around the Web to locate where those types of people tend to hang out. What blogs do they read (or would they read if they existed)? What communities do they belong to, if any? The answer could be "none," but if your product is new software, for example, you are going to find all kinds of communities. While you are reading through all the blogs, news sites, and communities, in the back of your mind you should ask yourself: How can we influence the folks on the Web who influence our prospects and customers? What you find in this observation step may surprise you.

Take consumer travel, for example. Say you market vacation packages. Based on your business's situation, your parameters might include a target audience of people 55 and older who have traveled outside the continental United States at least once in the past two years; English language sites; and three or four key potential destinations—Hong Kong, Shanghai, Kyoto, and Seoul. You might find (to your surprise and delight) that the thing people talk about most is currency conversion—how to do it, how to think about it. Currency conversion turns out to be a very hot topic. Conversations pop up about whether to bring traveler's checks, an ATM card, a credit card, a debit card, or convert money before leaving home. People want to know how much hard currency they should carry and what is the best place to find information on the exchange rates.

Now you've got an interesting insight. You started off wanting to know how best to reach consumers who are interested in traveling to the four destinations that you have chosen. Currency conversion turns out to be a major topic of interest. If your particular customers are talking about it, your company should become "the" source of information on the topic. Build a community of people who know about, have had experiences with, and can make suggestions about currency conversion. (I'll talk about these steps in the chapters ahead.)

Create a Customer Map

So far I've referred to a target market in terms of the prospective customers a company wants to reach to sell its products or services. But that, of course, is much too narrow a focus. A company of any size targets many customer groups interested in the organization (some authorities call these "stakeholders" or "constituents").

In this first step of observing the Web, you should identify who is saying what and which customer group they represent. A case in point is Saturn, which I used as an example early in this chapter. Saturn should be able to identify at least 10 customer groups: the people who buy the cars, the dealers who sell the cars, the service technicians who repair the cars, the finance people who finance the cars, the workers who build the cars, the regulators who rule on emissions and safety, insurance companies, parts suppliers, independent service shops, automotive writers/bloggers, and more.

While these are all specific and definable groups, they may overlap to some extent. An employee may also be a customer; a dealer may also handle the financing. Nevertheless, it is important to identify all these different customer groups and understand their wants, needs, and concerns, to create a customer map.

This is a key point. Customer communities are not limited to the folks who buy from you. Indeed, given your particular situation, your employees may be a more significant customer community to which you should be marketing. The community of your dealers may be able to offer each other more tips, ideas, and solutions than your own dealer relations people. It is important, therefore, that senior management map all these customer communities to ensure that no group is overlooked and that it ranks the groups periodically.

To sum up, the first step in understanding the social web for the marketer is observation. Don't stop at snorkeling. I often hear comments like, "Oh gee, my brand appeared in this blog or that blog. I Googled the company and I have this list of everything." That is snorkeling from the surface.

What I call observation involves diving deep into the social media and the blogosphere and understanding the most influential places within the social web world. You might find that Boing Boing is very popular with a *New York Times*-type reader and has more influence on the East Coast than in the Midwest and that it talks about these five topics. Or you might find that Gawker is important to teenage and young women. Or that theknot.com is particularly popular with young prospective brides. Or that yelp.com is reviewing restaurants, nightlife, shopping and more in New York, Chicago, San Francisco, Boston, and more.

Here's an example. You're a pharmaceutical company selling diabetes drugs and want to know the fastest growing, most important sites or blogs related to diabetes and diabetics. Which ones have the largest communities? What are the members talking about? What is the relevant content on a daily basis? How about the professional e-content of places like WebMD.com and Healthline.com? Much like the *New England Journal of Medicine*, there are digital versions of professional content.

You observe the blogosphere, the community sites, the forums, and other places where people are communicating with each other on the Web, and start looking for threads, topics, and places where people are commenting. You are definitely going to observe news events, the more traditional things that organizations have watched for years. But now you look for what is getting picked up and the chatter about it.

Once you have done the observation step ("done" rather than "finished," because in a sense it is never finished because the world continues to move), it's time to begin recruiting community members.

Step Two: Recruit Community Members

(With a New Toolbox and Your Own Marketing Skills)

D oes this sound familiar? "We tried a podcast . . . a microsite . . . a webinar, but nobody came. It was a waste of time and money." It's a complaint I often hear when I talk to executives about marketing to the social web.

Even when you observe what people are saying online about your brand and company, even when you map the various communities you want to attract, you can't just create an online presence and put out a sign saying: "Here we are." The "build it and they will come" strategy might have worked in the Internet 1.0 world of 1994, when web sites were still novelties (and unfortunately, some companies haven't abandoned this outdated strategy). But those days are gone forever.

Maybe it's a human impulse to believe that what's mine is better than what's yours, and companies fall into that trap just as individuals do. They believe that if they make a web site exciting, lively, colorful, and feature-rich, it will be better than other sites and attract attention. Your site may, in fact, be better, but so what? What's in it for the customer? The customer needs a real reason to show up. And that's where recruitment comes in.

Recruit as if Your Business Depends on It

Recruiting for the social web is serious business. Why? Because once people have been recruited to one or more communities, they tend to become impervious to further solicitation through traditional media. Consider these facts: According to the North American Technographics Benchmark Survey, Internet usage is going up while TV and radio usage are going down. Teens and twenty-something consumers already spend much more time online—and in social networks—than they do watching TV.[1] (That makes sense. A day still has only 24 hours, and the more time people spend online, the less time they have for other media.)

The impact of diminishing audiences is magnified by the increasing influence online communities have on the products and services their members buy. Nearly 75 percent of the people who spend time online say their friends and family are the primary influence on their purchase decisions, and 63 percent consider reviews and product comparisons from other consumers to be as credible as expert reviews from independent third parties.

This trend of using the social web to inform buying decisions and circumventing marketing messages is sure to continue and spread. More than one-third of consumers said in a recent study that in the future they will rely on product reviews found through forums and online networks more frequently. Nine out of ten Internet users say they put a lot more trust in what online contacts say than in what advertisers or retailers say.[2] And 20 percent of consumers say that, based on information found online, they purchased a different product than the one they originally intended to buy.[3]

If you don't recruit people, if you don't engage them with meaningful content, you'll get run over by the speeding locomotive the social web has become. Only by recruiting members and getting your site ready for community can you put the power of the social web to work for your business goals.

Bring a New Toolkit to the Job

At the start of this chapter, I mentioned an all-too-common lament: a company opened its site and nobody came. Let me suggest two reasons why people might not come to your online party. First, there was little or no outreach to the social web; and second, the content was not compelling enough. You need a definite plan for attracting and retaining community members. And that's where your marketing knowledge and skills come in.

Marketing to the social web does *not* mean forgetting everything you've learned. It does mean using a new toolkit or approach to build on what you already know. You'll need new and different perspectives on how you connect with and relate to consumers, but the basics of good strategic and tactical marketing communications don't change. You're trying to generate leads, produce revenue, and exert influence; you're trying to generate brand awareness, induce trial, and build customer loyalty. It's the old lather, rinse, and repeat from Marketing 101.

None of this is particularly revolutionary, but it's absolutely critical. You already have some idea of how to address many of the questions raised by marketing to the social web. Now it's time to put your skills to work by recruiting members for your online community.

You recruit online community members the same way you do in the offline world, but it is much easier and richer online. A good starting place is to think about the reasons why people join online communities at all. According to Compete Inc.,[4] there are four reasons:

1. *Meet people.* Some 78 percent of the people who visit online communities join them to communicate with others, either colleagues or new acquaintances with whom they develop relationships.

2. *Entertain themselves.* Another 47 percent join to find entertaining content such as photos, music, or videos.

3. *Learn something new.* Some 38 percent join because they want to obtain information about topics that hold particular interest to them.

4. *Influence others.* And 23 percent join to express their opinions in a forum where their ideas can be discussed, debated, or acted on.

Note: These add up to more than 100 percent because some people participate for two or more reasons.

Send Out Your Invitations

With these four reasons in mind, you can start crafting an approach to recruiting members to your community. Perhaps the simplest and most direct place to begin is with the names and addresses available in company databases. These may come from warranty cards, contest entries, dealer lists—any source your firm has used in the past to build a mailing list.

Another simple recruiting technique is to print the site's URL on product labels and invite people to join. You should certainly include the URL in all your printed company marketing materials—catalogs, brochures, direct mail, and advertisements.

You can buy a list from a research panel company much the way you would buy a list for a direct mail effort from a list broker. These are opt-in lists of people who have chosen to receive e-mail communications (which distinguishes this approach from spam). Send those people an invitation to join your community. Your e-mail invitation has to be as engaging and attractive as any direct mail piece. Be sure that when people respond, they find themselves taken to a web site where they would like to be. Otherwise, with a click, you'll be added to the spam filter.

More broadly, recruiting to the social web consists of two toolkits: digital media marketing and digital media relations. Digital media marketing creates branded community-based destinations and invites people to come to them through the sources I've just mentioned and through paid advertising. These destinations could be webisodes (cartoons or a short film—often in installments—used to promote offline events or products), microsites (a web site developed with a particular focus for a specific target audience), a contest, or a viral experience. Digital media marketing can cover the spectrum from kooky viral videos to very serious targeted microsites that might be targeted at a very narrow (or not so narrow) target audience that you want to reach with your product or service.

As an example, the site 43things.com has found an interesting way to build communities. The site invites visitors to list things they would like to do with their lives: Improve my vocabulary . . . practice yoga . . . backpack through Europe...have a secret underground lair . . . the list is endless. "It's more like a life list than a to-do list," says John Peterson, one of the site's seven founders. "It's not about the 10 things I want to do this week; it's more about the 10 most important things in my life that I never write on my to-do list."

What makes the site interesting is that when you create your list, you are automatically connected to everyone else within the 43 Things universe who want to accomplish those same goals. At that point, you can write to those people and they can write to you; you can share ideas, setbacks, and successes. In other words, just by expressing your goal, you join the community. If "lose weight" is your goal, your community can include the 30,521 other 43 Things participants who share that goal.

Think of digital media relations as next generation public relations. It has the same goal as traditional public relations—to engage in and influence conversation in a prescribed channel. In the digital world, these are online spheres of influence, which include reputation aggregators, blogs, e-communities, and social networks. The approach you use in digital media relations is somewhat different from the approach used in traditional public relations, because the digital channel is, to some extent, disintermediated by the online spheres of influence.

In offline public relations, firms have to work through the traditional print and broadcast channels. They have to get to know the right writers, reporters, and editors, the right analysts. They have to know the people who influence or decide what newspapers and magazines publish and radio and television stations broadcast. Online the process is similar, but digital media relations have five major differences. They are:

1. *Interactive*. Digital media relations is interactive with many voices involved in the discussion; this contrasts with traditional PR which was a one-way broadcast from media to public.

2. *Immediate*. There are no deadlines, a response can be instantaneous; this is very different from the lead times that traditional media require.

3. *Interconnected*. The content can be aggregated, shared, linked, and pushed out.

4. *Inclusive*. People who have common interests and passions can easily gather and discuss and share their concerns.

5. *Infinite*. There are no limitations on an audience; publish on the web locally and distribution is global.

If digital media relations means influencing opinions, attitudes, or behaviors, how you go about it depends on the channel, the goals, the product or service, and the company life cycle. What is your marketing goal? How you recruit community members depends on the business objective for starting the community, both the near-term and long-term business objectives.

Create That Community Feeling

I asked Tom Gerace, the founder and CEO of Gather.com, about companies starting online communities. Gather.com is a community where engaged, informed adults can connect over everything from food to politics to travel to gardening to health to money to movies and much more. Members can express opinions, ask questions, post pictures, rate articles, and form subgroups.

Should marketers expect that if they build an online community, people will show up and participate? Tom says, "I think in most cases they won't. It's not just the technology. The social networking platform is a critical component, of course, but equally important is the community and the quality of the experience that members of the community create for other members. So, when marketers think about launching social networks, they need to ask: Why would people want to form community around this place, this brand, or whatever it happens to be? There are very few brands that people feel such affinity for that they want to link their personal identity to the brand in a persistent way. And few people feel connected to other human beings because of their mutual affinity to a particular brand."

Of course there always exceptions. Harley Davidson comes to mind as a brand/product around which owners will gather. Another example: Lego Group, which promotes the Lego Ambassadors as a community-based program in which adult Lego hobbyists share their construction, product, and event knowledge with the worldwide Lego community. They are not employees, but "contribute to the Lego fan community without the promise, expectation, or receipt of compensation. The Lego Ambassadors Program is an officially recognized community based program of the Lego Group."[5]

But does someone who uses, say, a Macintosh computer want to socialize with other Mac owners—online or offline—just because they all own Apple products? Probably not. They're unlikely to go out of their way to find other Mac owners, unless they're true geeks, the 2 or 3 percent of owners who absolutely love Apple and its products.

Jeep encourages community feeling by trying to get owners to wave to other Jeep owners. "I am actually a Jeep owner myself," says Tom, "and I love going off-road. But do I want to meet other Jeep owners? No, I want to be with my four friends in the Jeep."

Gather.com suggests that, rather than trying to climb the very steep hill of convincing consumers to form some social relationship around the brand identity itself, agencies and advertisers participate in existing social spaces. "Marketers need to get their minds around the idea that the social space is inherently different from traditional media," Tom explains. He points out that in the social space, content comes from trusted, known sources. This confirms your own experience: You know whom you believe for anything from a movie recommendation to a book recommendation to introductions to other people to job references. So in a social space, the content is almost guaranteed to be relevant and to be trusted if you believe the people are trustworthy (or you don't listen to them).

"Because you have exceptionally high degrees of relevance and trust," says Tom, "other people trust the content you place in the social networks as a result. The question is: Do you feel the same level of affinity or trust or love for a brand that you do for another individual? I think the answer is no. Can a brand build that level of affinity? Probably not. Brands don't give love."

In his view, what is driving the social web and why people spend so much time on these sites—a point that many marketers haven't yet grasped—is that people benefit from exploring the lives of friends, family, colleagues, and strangers with similar interests and concerns. The explosive growth of social media such as MySpace reflects that benefit; they have a huge reach right now and their reach is still growing. As a result, Tom advises that companies get involved not by building a community around the brand but by "going into established, successful communities and creating value, which will tend to attract more people to the community."

Diane Hessan, the founder and CEO of Communispace Corp., brings up another key issue to consider when recruiting members: "In general, it's harder to recruit people for a community involving a low-involvement product or service than for a high-involvement product." Communispace develops collaborative online communities for company clients—more than 300 at this writing—as a way to connect marketers and customers and provoke insights that companies can use.

In Diane's experience, the issue of involvement affects recruiting for all kinds of products and brands. "If a client said to us, 'We need people who fly on airlines a lot and who want to be in an airline community,' it would be a lot easier to establish that community than, say, a toilet paper community," she says. "As it turns out, a lot of companies in the toilet paper business want to build communities and understand their customers, so we finally figured out a number of things that must be done to recruit people to these communities. It's not rocket science, but you have to be thoughtful. Sometimes companies lose perspective and they think, 'Oh, wow, what we do is so important and so interesting, people will want to be part of our community.'"

Diane also points out that even when people register at your site, they may not actually continue in the community: "Sometimes people will sign up, go in, decide it's really boring, and not participate any further. In the meantime, the company is saying, 'We have one million visitors!'"

To sum up, you're facing a two-part challenge: recruiting people to the site in the first place and keeping them engaged once you get them there. I'll be talking about the second part in the next chapter.

Build on Existing Sites and Communities

Instead of trying to form an entirely new community around your brand—which is clearly very tough to do—you might start a community to add appeal to a web site you already have. Let's say you're in the travel business and you've set up a microsite for enthusiasts interested in traveling to sporting events around the world—World Cup Soccer, Olympic Games, World Figure Skating Championships. How could you build community around this microsite?

First, link your site to the event's official web site as well as to other relevant sports sites; for figure skating, these might be sites such as isu.org and goldenskate.com. A part of the online experience for this target segment is going to be a community where people can share content about destinations, content that can be text, photos, and video. Your links will help people find and exchange this kind of information. They'll also serve to recruit members in an indirect way.

Next, locate experts on figure skating and travel to the host city (this year, it's in Los Angeles). Look for folks who have something material and interesting to say. Maybe they're knowledgeable about the sport and the skaters, or they've closely followed winners of previous skating championships. Find people who have special—and up-to-date—information about places to stay and eat in and around the area. Your experts should be able to offer advice about getting around the country, interesting side trips, and so on.

It helps to put yourself in the shoes of someone who's interested in the content of your microsite. If you cared enough about the World Figure Skating Championships or the sport of figure skating, you probably would visit the site every few days or once a week to see what's new. Maybe someone has posted an interesting comment or quote; maybe another member has reacted to something you posted. And if you spotted special travel offers or other offers on the site, you might check those every now and then. You might return if you found occasional interviews with athletes or coaches—even with the athletes' families.

Now think about the microsite as a whole, not just the skating enthusiasts. Recruit 10 or 20 experts in each of the several geographies where upcoming international-level sporting events will be held. They'll be community members but clearly identified as experts. You *must* be transparent so that if your experts have a relationship with an event, a hotel, a restaurant, or anything else they discuss, this must be very clear to site visitors.

You'll want to have compelling content for seeding until the site gets enough momentum to meet your business objective. The level of that momentum will differ depending on your business purpose. This is why you'll need a marketing plan, a course of action, for obtaining content and building momentum to attract and engage your customers and prospects.

Feel the Momentum

One good way to get momentum going is by seeding your community with quality content that inspires people to talk up the information and the site to others. In any community, you're going to have participants and lurkers—folks who visit the site but never ask a question or post a comment. The lurkers are important, too. A lurker may take an action that is important for the overall objectives at some point—she may book a tour for example—and lurkers may tell friends about the site, encouraging those people to visit and participate actively.

Other ways to recruit are the good old-fashioned ways. Remember the principle of don't forget what you already know. You want to look at the business case for online advertising, offline advertising, traditional public relations, online public relations or digital media relations, paid search, and more. Getting people to come to your community and then return again and again means you must have something they care about enough to come back for. It's as simple and as hard as that.

What other sites do you need to go to for recruiting purposes? What kind of paid media should be used? Perhaps you should buy ads on Google to bring people to your community. As I've said before, the Web allows you to measure your advertising's effectiveness and you can see the most important places your customers come from and go to.

Planning for recruitment requires a mindset. Ask yourself: Which are the most powerful media? Where are my customers going? Where are my competitors? Here's an analogy: When advertisers created a 30-second commercial, the agency had to think about the lighting and the music, the movement, the message, and the logo. For a web site, you do the same kind of thing. You're developing an environment that will present information, allow for interactivity, draw like-minded people, and create transactions. You're not creating marketing material, you're creating a digital environment.

Does direct marketing online have a role in marketing to the social web? Does public relations online have a role? Does paid advertising have a role online? Yes, yes, and yes. But the goal of all those tactical, executable things is to create a theater of sales, and to bring people to rich, thoughtful, interesting online communities.

And once you've brought them to your community, what can you do to keep them coming back?

Step Three: Evaluate Online Conduit Strategies

(And Don't Forget Search)

W ho do you want to reach? What do you want to say to them? Those are the key questions to think about as you plan your conduit strategies—your plan for using the social web to reach your target audiences. The big four conduit strategies are reputation aggregators, blogs, e-communities, and social networks.

And don't forget search, for the simple reason that you want people to find *you*, whether they're using a desktop PC, laptop, or mobile device like an iPhone. Search comes in two flavors: unpaid—or organic—and paid. Both can offer a nice return, especially when you give people multiple ways to find you. Consider the experience of the U.K. travel company MyTravel, part of the Thomas Cook Group.

MyTravel hired a search-marketing agency to research destination-specific search terms and more general search terms that people use when gathering vacation information online. The agency indexed the corresponding key terms on every MyTravel page so the most relevant content would show up in search engine results. It also set up a MyTravel channel on YouTube and prepared branded video travel guides optimized for easy searching. Adding a MyTravel vacation blog and travel reviews helped catapult more of the company's links high in search results.

The bottom line: MyTravel's sales from organic search have grown by nearly 400 percent, conversion is up 65 percent, and spending on paid search is down.[1] You can see that it really pays to think about search.

This Way to the Conduit

Before I explain the big four in more detail, I want to emphasize that the lines of demarcation between reputation aggregators, blogs, e-communities, and social networks are somewhat permeable. The line between e-community and social network can blur, meaning it's hard to say where an e-community ends and a social network begins. The line between blog and reputation aggregator is definitely blurry: Important blogs and the links they cite are very important, and so the blogs themselves are reputation aggregators targeted at a relatively narrow audience. The bottom line: Conduit strategies are not black and white.

Now a bit more about the big four conduit strategies. (This chapter paints the big picture; in Part III, I'll detail how you can actually use each of them effectively.)

1. A reputation aggregator is a site that provides rankings of content/sites. People use these sites to decide what content they want or need. The way in which the ranking is done varies very widely. Some use keyword algorithms to measure popularity (Google, Yahoo!, Ask, and MSN among others); others use member/visitor comments/reviews (Yelp—restaurants, hotels,

shopping in major cities; AngiesList—home improvement companies in local markets; and TripAdvisor—resorts, hotels, travel packages). How high a site appears in a search result influences the site's reputation.

2. A blog (or web log, although only pedants call them that these days) is a digital diary; authors post dated journal entries (with or without video, photos, illustrations, and links to other blogs, other sites) that readers can comment on.

3. E-communities are online sites where people aggregate around a common interest area with topical interest and often includes professional content. Examples include Sermo for physicians, IT Toolbox for IT people, and CafeMom for mothers.

4. Social networks are member-based communities that enable users to link to one another through invites. Examples include Facebook, MySpace, Orkut, GenForum, LinkedIn, and many, many more.

The *social web*, by the way, covers all four conduits. Also bear in mind that the conduits will continue to change, just as what was considered a web site in 1993 would hardly be considered a web site today.

Another point: Marketing, advertising, and public relations people often talk about "platforms." There are really two platforms: the actual physical or electronic platform—a television set, a newspaper, a magazine, the Internet, and even sites like salesforce.com, mzinga. com, kickapps.com, and others—and the communications platform—what you're trying to say.

To be clear, this chapter is about the online conduits you can use to communicate your platform, not the electronic platforms themselves. The communications platform involves analyzing who you're trying to reach and what you're trying to say. So think about questions like: What do we stand for? What is our position in the marketplace? What are the messages we want to get out to our various customer communities? Is our audience more interested in listening to things than reading about them? Are they more visual, interested in seeing a lot of things? Do they want their questions answered? Do they want to comment about, say, a drug's side effects, a computer's performance, or a politician's behavior?

Again, you don't need to forget everything you already know as a marketer. You're not starting from scratch when you market to the social web. You're just adding some new sensibilities and perspectives to your toolkit.

Searching, Searching

As you formulate conduit strategies, consider how search engines (which act as a form of reputation aggregator) rank sites. The rankings can vary widely based on a site's age, content, keywords, structure, and links to other sites. In addition, think about how prospects, customers, partners, financial analysts, and other people might go about finding your product or company online.

Because some percentage of these people will find you using search engines, you can't ignore where your site comes up in the search results. The good news is that you can materially affect search results using unpaid media, such as blogs, e-communities, and social networks, as MyTravel did. Jefferson Graham, a USA Today reporter, interviewed Matt Cutts, a Google engineer, to learn ways to make a site easier to find. Cutts had five suggestions:

1. Spotlight your search term on the page.
2. Fill in your "tags."
3. Get other sites to link back to you.
4. Create a blog and post often.
5. Register for free tools. Google's google.com/webmaster offers free help to get your site found.[2]

While search engine optimization has become an entire special discipline, the principles of organic search are fairly straightforward. Identify the hot topics and search terms that people are likely to use to find you. If prospective customers are not deeply familiar with your product or solution, they're not going to hunt for it. So try to imagine what they *will* hunt for and "tag" your site so it turns up. (A tag is a word or code assigned to items like Web pages or photos to facilitate searching and sharing. "Bahamas hotel" could be a tag.) If your site is not turning up on search results or is far down in the rankings, you have to start using the other three conduits as well as digital media marketing, otherwise known as paid search.

Your goal is to create branded community-based destinations to start the virtuous circle in motion: a person finds your site, comments, links to it, tells friends and acquaintances who tell their friends and acquaintances who link back to your site, and so it goes. And as the circle grows, your site moves higher and higher in the rankings.

A few words about mobile search: Remember that the screen is so small that customers may not know about you if your site isn't at or near the top of the results. You might want to consider paid mobile search, which is growing incredibly fast as people migrate to smart phones and the like. According to Christian Hernandez Gallardo, head of Google's distribution partnerships, publishers are particularly interested in paid keyword mobile-search ads. "Much like on the web, they're working to improve their presence on mobile. The difference is that discovering content is a lot harder on mobile. Consumers don't want to browse, they want to find."[3]

That's why specialized mobile search is blossoming. NearbyNow, for instance, lets shoppers text to find discounts and check the inventory of nearby stores for pinpoint shopping. Help customers find exactly what they want, when and where they want it, and they're more likely to buy from *you*.

More about Blogs

You hear a lot these days about blogs and the blogosphere, a collective term encompassing all blogs as a community or social network. Many blogs are densely interconnected; bloggers read others' blogs, link to them, reference them in their own writing, and post comments on each others' blogs. Since a blog is also a web site, the term "site" and "blog" can sometimes be used interchangeably if a site has blog capabilities.

Is blogging right for your company or brand? Consider what role you want it to play. Do you want to play a thought leadership role? If so, blogging is probably a really good idea. Here's the big but: Blogging is a good conduit strategy only if you can imagine you or someone in the company becoming a publisher with an editorial calendar, an editorial agenda, and—guess what?—a writer.

The hard part is becoming a publisher with the responsibility for obtaining content, enforcing deadlines, and maintaining quality. This is very similar to Web 1.0 in the early 1990s when an executive might wake up one day and say, "I need a web site and it has to go live in six weeks." And in 1993 or 1994—maybe 1995 for latecomers—the site might go up without the company figuring out how to keep the thing fed, fresh, new. The blogosphere is very similar—you have to be a publisher and publish regularly to make any impact at all.

If you can't commit to an editorial agenda and calendar, with an editorial strategy that supports your overall marketing goal, don't do it. If you're only going to post every six weeks, or every six months, don't bother. Don't wind up like the failures of Web 1.0, when people looked at a web site, saw that it hadn't changed for weeks or months, and decided the company was either sleepy or clueless.

I'm still shocked when I visit a web site, check out the company's press releases and links to news stories, and see that the most recent item is eight months old. Is the firm still in business? Are its managers so busy that they have no time to update the web site? Has nothing newsworthy happened in eight months?

Don't set up an online newsroom if you can't maintain it; otherwise, the company looks moribund. Keeping a newsroom or company blog current requires an investment in time. Not only do you have the initial cost of setting up the mechanism, you have to consider the ongoing cost to maintain, whether internal time or an outside consultant's time and fee.

Nevertheless, as Jonathan Schwartz, the president and chief operating officer at Sun Microsystems, has said, "Leadership is all about communications, it's what leaders do. Almost by definition, your set of responsibilities comes down to who you pick to work for you, how much budget you give them, and then what do you say all day long when you are trying to motivate change and drive people forward. So blogging is a tool that, especially for leaders, is critical to amplify your communications."[4]

Welcome to the E-Community

E-communities offer content to members and allow member (or visitor) dialogue. In addition to the sites I mentioned earlier in the chapter, sites like IBM.com, Cisco.com, Sun.com, and Microsoft.com contain e-communities within them in which developers, customers, and partners can ask questions and share answers. No hard sell, but lots of interesting information. In addition to professional e-communities, there are communities focusing on health, food, wine, sports, cars, travel, and more.

Here's where your marketing smarts come into play. You need to clarify your marketing objectives and determine whether an e-community would help achieve these goals. If so, go ahead and create the site—with concrete plans for maintaining it. On the other hand, maybe you don't need a separate e-community. Depending on your situation and objectives, would you benefit more from participating in someone else's existing e-community?

Just as Welch's Grape Jelly might team up with Skippy Peanut Butter in a joint promotion and L.L. Bean has linked with Subaru, so could a pharmaceutical company team up with Sermo.com ("created by physicians, for physicians") or a pet food company with Dogster. com. In fact, 3M's Scotch Fur Fighter Hair Remover recently sponsored America's Furriest Friend Photo Contest on Dogster, inviting community members to post photos of their furry dogs and vote for the furriest. The contest page included a quick product demo video, three bullets with product benefits, and a link to more product information. This is the kind of targeted promotion that gets a lot of bark for the buck.

If you are a small company, you can search not just in these big-time online e-communities, but small trade groups—restaurants, opticians, liquor stores, specialty shops, all depending on your local market or trading area. But on e-communities, you are not only aware but can give opinions and answer questions.

Tap into Social Networks

Certain social networks—MySpace, Facebook, Twitter, YouTube—have received a huge amount of publicity, but there are actually hundreds more online. Nearly all require members to register, and some—like aSmallWorld, DeadJournal, and Doostang—require an invitation to join. You can market on a social network, but be very careful in the approach you take. In fact, before you jump in, study what other companies have done.

For instance, some companies are getting their brands in front of audiences through fun applications that work with social networks. SuperPoke is an application that lets Facebook friends give each other, well, a little online poke (or some other animated action). Estee Lauder recently sponsored a SuperPoke that squirted virtual perfume at the recipient. It didn't have or need a big marketing message; what it did have was a fun association with the brand.

You can't release a major movie today without having a presence on Facebook, MySpace, YouTube, or other popular social networks. What if you're marketing hardware or software, financial services or healthcare? Should you market on these venues? My advice is to be very prudent. Remember, "build it and they will come" does not apply online. "Blow it and they will slam you," however, definitely applies.

Signs of a backlash are now turning up. For example, a columnist for *The Telegraph* in the U.K. writes, "As time-wasting opportunities go, no one in history has come up with anything to match YouTube. Every day starts the same: switch on the computer, check the email inbox, then follow the links to YouTube that have been sent by various correspondents eager to share their discoveries. . . . And the thing is, long before you have clocked on to what is happening, you are being manoeuvred into position by somebody trying to sell you something. . . . These days, not only are we wasting endless time but in every second of it we are being manipulated."[5]

Perhaps the biggest challenge of the online world is the speed with which news, ideas, and opinions can catch on virally—both positive and negative. So choose your social networks with great care.

Step Four: Engage Communities in Conversation

(To Generate Word of Mouse)

Up to this point, you've observed the field and created a customer map, recruited community members, and evaluated online conduit strategies. Now it's time to plan to engage your community (or communities) in conversation. Approach this as if you were writing a marketing plan with the target audience of customers and potential customers in mind. Your conduit strategies will guide many of the activities you plan. Of course a web site (or more than one) will be part of your plan and of course it must have great content—"great," that is, *as defined by your target audience.*

How do you engage a community in conversation? Before I talk about the nuts and bolts, I want to show you a company that understands its target audience and has a variety of conversation starters in its toolkit.

Bubbly Conversation

Jones Soda Co., based in Seattle, Washington, has been building a community conversation for years. First, a little background. If you haven't seen Jones Soda at your local Starbucks or Panera Bread, you may not know that the company differentiates itself by cooking up some very quirky flavors. For the holidays, it has offered limited-edition flavors such as Turkey and Gravy soda, Christmas Ham soda, and Latke soda. Year-round flavors include Strawberry Manilow, Blue Bubblegum, and Your Momegranate.

Just looking at the soda is enough to start a conversation because the photos and sayings on each bottle have been submitted by customers (and sometimes by employees). But how do customers get into the conversation? Check the label, and you'll see the Jones URL (jonessoda.com). Now conversation is just a click away.

Jones involves customers in its brand and promotes a conversation in at least a dozen ways. Under the web site's "community" tab are some very good examples. On the message board, for instance, "members" (visitors who log in) can post comments about Jones's products, its special events, and—gasp!—subjects that have nothing whatever to do with Jones. The guest book is exactly what it sounds like: a page where visitors can sign in and leave a quick note for Jones—a simple yet welcoming touch.

To backtrack to that label, customers who upload a photo or a saying through the web site are more likely to visit regularly so they can find out whether their submission has been chosen. In fact, Jones encourages visitors to browse an ever-changing gallery of photos and sayings on the site itself. Although this may sound one-sided (customers submit and Jones picks), it actually generates dialogue because visitors get to vote on the best photo of the year. Jones also encourages customers to rate and review its individual flavors and to suggest new flavors. These are good conversation starters.

The web site has timely games and promotions to bring visitors back again and again. Last year, its Campaign Cola 2008 page offered three special-edition colas, one with Barack Obama's face on the label, one with John McCain's face, and one with Hillary Clinton's face. Visitors were exhorted to "cast your vote early for the 2008 presidential election. There's no limit to how many times you can vote; here at Jones you can buy your candidate's way to victory." (The cost of buying victory: $14.99 per six pack.) Non-buyers got their two cents in by posting messages to the page's forum.

How about some direct customer feedback? The "Contact us" page—a must-have for every site—lets visitors tell Jones exactly what they think or ask questions. They can also sign up for the company's e-newsletter to stay updated on promotions, new flavors, and more.

Here's my point: Jones does all this not just to sell soda pop but also to engage customers and potential customers in a dialogue.

A Brand Is a Dialogue

In the era of the social web, branding is the dialogue you have with your customers and potential customers. The stronger the dialogue, the stronger the brand; the weaker the dialogue, the weaker the brand. Thanks to the Internet, the dialogue can be active 24 hours a day, 365 days a year. It includes both the conversations you have with customers and the exchanges your customers have with one another—all related to the strength of the brand.

Apple is terrifically strong on the social web by encouraging conversation around its brand. Apple dominates portable music with the iPod and its siblings. Some of the iPod-like devices made by other companies are just as good if not better than the iPod, yet Apple owns 75 percent of that market because it keeps the dialogue going with its customers. Do you want the user experience to be faster? Do you want the machine smaller or more stylish? Do you want a better screen? Do you want to watch television shows? Movies? This kind of dialogue contributes to Apple's amazing brand power. It's not the only communication Apple has with its community: the company also uses traditional marketing and advertising to bring people into the online conversation.

Apple is good at building dialogue around product enhancement and user-experience, which in turn strengthens its brand. Another way to stimulate conversation is to use a moral purpose—renewable energy, fair prices for coffee growers, children's health, automotive safety, and the like—as the starting point.

Stonyfield Farm, for example, is deeply concerned about environmental issues. Known for organic and natural food products like yogurt, smoothies, and soy milk, Stonyfield mentions its pet causes on product labels and is always posting new content on its web site (stonyfield.com). It has something to say about global warming, healthy eating, sustainable agriculture, supporting family farms, and much more. And it wants to hear what customers think.

The Baby Babble blog on the Stonyfield site presents content by and for parents interested in ideas about raising children. The Bovine Bugle blog, about daily life on an all-organic Vermont farm, also generates its share of interesting comments from the community. People who gravitate toward the Stonyfield community for its causes can get involved by reading site content, voting on which nonprofits should receive Stonyfield's donations, and following links to various advocacy organizations. All this for a mass-market consumer packaged good.

Even though Groupe Danone has a majority stake in Stonyfield, the brand has a distinct, independent identity because it keeps the conversation going on so many levels. When Stonyfield celebrated its 25th anniversary, it invited customers to help "co-create some significant changes in our product offerings and our packaging look, as well as our web site and newsletter content." The company sweetened the deal by offering a month's supply of yogurt to 100 people who signed up to participate in this more intensive dialogue.

Let me make another point here: Company executives should stop thinking that they can buy a brand name or build a great brand simply by making big media buys. Neither Stonyfield nor Jones is buying a lot of media space or time, yet each brand has a sizable community of loyal followers. True, most managers in senior positions today grew up with the Super Bowl mentality—buy enough advertising and you create the brand. Those days are gone; I don't think any company can buy its way into a brand name anymore. The increasing importance of social media and social marketing on the Web is, I believe, tipping the balance and will have much more impact than media buys.

One more key point about making conversation in a community: Don't talk about what Merck stands for, or what Coke stands for, or what any brand stands for. You have to show this (like Stonyfield) and get a dialogue going. What does your company care about—from a social nature, from a moral nature, from an ethical nature? That is the high-level part of a branding dialogue. Then you have to do the every-day work of carrying on a dialogue about specific issues surrounding the products and services you offer. Stonyfield does this with its invitation for the community to share ideas about products, packaging, newsletters, and more.

Remember the days when TV commercials actually demonstrated a product's strengths and benefits? I suggest you go back to the future by reinventing demonstrations as part of community conversations. Blendtec, a blender company with a double-digit marketing budget, is a master at this.

How tough are Blendtec blenders? To see for yourself, click on any of its entertaining "Will It Blend?" videos, which are all over YouTube as well as the Blendtec site and WillItBend.com. As the CEO uses a Blendtec to pulverize all kinds of unlikely objects, from an iPhone to a handful of marbles, his low key commentary only adds to the humor. Seeing is believing, which is why Blendtec videos have been viewed some 60 million times.

Community members can get in on the fun in several ways. They can submit suggestions for objects to be blended or test their own blenders (safely) on "try this at home" materials recommended by Blendtec. They can follow along on the Will It Blog as the company cooks up new blending challenges and add their thoughts. And they can share their favorite Blendtec videos with one click. Now you're asking "Will it sell?" The answer is yes: Blendtec's retail sales quintupled in the first year after starting to post videos.

Making Customers Part of the Brand

Customers have always played a small role in the world of the brand, as research subjects, as enthusiasts, and as gadflies. Today, however, because of the Internet, you have to think of customers as transmitters of your brand conversation. They're already having conversations with one another about your products anyway, conversations about your cars or your music or your drug's side effects. It's up to you to ensure that your organization participates in that conversation and convinces community members that you care about what they think and say about the brand, products, and services.

What customers and potential customers talk about is deeply connected to your reputation and your position as a brand in the social media world. That's why you have to be part of the dialogue, no matter what brand you market. If you market flat screen television sets—although the product or service could be virtually anything—how do you contribute to the dialogue about, say, advancements in flat panel technology? One way you might participate is by explaining what makes a good flat panel screen, on your web site and in other online forums.

You need to add your voice to the conversation in places where you can participate in transparent fashion, so it's clear who you are and who you represent. At the same time, you should link back and invite people to your site for more dialogue or an opportunity for visitors to just listen, for instance, to a podcast about the quality elements in flat panel screens (or whatever is meaningful to your audience). You might offer videos of your product in use (like Blendtec) or in development, allow the community to see the results of product testing, or have your service people post tips and answer questions. The more your customers are involved in the dialogue, the more they get involved in the brand.

Because a branded dialogue should be multidimensional, think about building a conversation around what you stand for, based on your activities. For example, British Petroleum's Beyond Petroleum campaign was more than just advertising. It was a discussion about renewable energy, a great first step to set British Petroleum apart from other big oil companies. BP also compiles an annual Statistical Review of World Energy showing both consumption and production—another great way to generate conversation. Similarly, Pfizer has stimulated dialogues about different diseases, with the implied message that "we are trying to make a higher quality of life for you; this is what we're about—not just making money." Remove the subject of transactions and profit from the brand dialogue and you actually add another dimension to the dialogue.

The dialogue, after all, changes to fit the community's interest. Does the ordinary customer care if General Motors makes money? Some may, but most care about a new vehicle. Does General Motors offer fuel-efficient cars at good prices? Do people like them? Are they reliable? Most prospective customers don't care what the stock is worth. A portfolio manager at Fidelity cares, and they care about a different brand dialogue or brand conversation.

The future of the Web is going to be about branded destinations, which include social networks. What do I mean by branded destinations?

The Motley Fool (fool.com) is a branded destination. The Fool Community (that's actually a page on the site) offers a variety of suggestions and advice from community members covering everything from investment strategies to food and drink, financial planning to health and fitness. Members of the community, who must register to participate, can log on and ask for help. iVillage.com is a branded destination, as is Gather.com. I would even argue that any site, after it reaches a certain critical mass, can be considered a branded destination.

The next generation of branded Web destinations will be designed as a place to aggregate, supported by advertising. Look at Eons.com, founded by Jeff Taylor, who founded the Monster.com job site. Eons is sort of a MySpace for baby boomers. Members (and you have to be at least 50 or lie about your age to become a member) can share life dreams, calculate life expectancy, follow news stories about aging, and much more. The site carries advertising, sponsored discussion groups, and branded games. Recent ads I noticed were for Ott-Lite lamps, a Humana Medicare plan, and the LavaLife Prime mature dating site. A recent game was a word search sponsored by the Microsoft Live Search Club.

In addition, remember that the social web filters transactions. The Eons site is an example of this. The chances are good that someone who clicks from Eons to the LavaLife Prime ad or the Humana Medicare plan ad is a good prospect for a dating service or an insurance plan that targets seniors.

These—and hundreds of other sites—are social interfaces that may lead to a transaction, versus sites that simply offer transactions, which is where the Web has been for the past 10 years. It is the difference between going to a site to buy things and going to a site for an experience and *then* buying. In the future, branding will be built more on experience and discussion about the experience, although traditional advertising and promotion will still have some influence. For some leading brands, the future is now. Dialogues about experiences are already shaping and reinforcing what community members think, feel, say, and do about these brands.

Ordinarily it takes a long time to build a brand, but the social web has shown this is not always true. It took Google about eight years to become a verb. YouTube did not spend a dime on advertising and became a national brand in less than three years. iVillage has become a brand for information for women. MySpace, BlackPlanet, hulu, and more have become brand names almost overnight.

How did that happen? Through the dialogue on the sites and the conversations visitors have with each other, the brands became strong. Not just dialogue but also the fulfillment of a promise made through that dialogue, either by offering information a visitor wants or by getting to the product through the information. Brands will become more and more powerful as they fulfill the promise made in their dialogues with customers and the dialogues among customers.

Any brand that tries to game the system or has a shoddy product or shady proposal will be found out more quickly and punished more severely on the social web. The super-duper Kryptonite bike lock (which someone discovered could be picked by a Bic pen and broadcast how on the Web) and the "Dell Hell" service problems are just two examples of how Web-savvy consumers can, and will, turn on a company they feel has not done the right thing.

Too Much of a Good Thing

As the social web grows and customers get on board, they'll vary their participation in what I see as three tiers of communities:

1. The first tier of communities are built around what customers talk most about, care most about—school, profession, disease, hobby, sports passion, dating service.

2. The second tier of communities are those that customers will visit now and then. These may not be as important or immediate as the first tier but they're of enough interest to warrant an occasional visit.

3. The third tier of communities are where customers go when they have something specific in mind. Maybe they're thinking about an annual vacation, a refinanced mortgage, a presidential election. Customers aren't always looking for travel tips, but when they're getting ready for their one big trip of the year, they might visit three community sites to look for interesting places.

A customer may buy many different branded products, but they'll only belong to a limited number of communities on the social web, perhaps 10 or 12. Moreover, many of these communities may have only marginal connection to commerce. Over time, people will most likely perform triage on their community involvement. Some will belong to subcommunities; they may not be directly in dialogue with the company, but will be comfortable with the company. For example, someone may trust Stonyfield and will continue to watch the company's site now and then or dip in and out of the community maybe once a month or so, just as shoppers like to drop into certain stores at irregular intervals.

Once the novelty of the social web wears off, people will become more selective. For example, Aarica Caro, a 28-year-old escrow officer who lives in Morgan Hill, California, has shared enough. She's shared a list of her favorite television shows and movies, reviews of Bay Area haunts, and she's been invited to share more. She was invited to join other online communities such as Yahoo 360, but she didn't bother to sign up. She said her MySpace page is enough. "It's getting pretty old," Caro said. "It makes no sense to have a million of those pages. I have one."

For a while, Caro shared the lives of her three cats on Catster.com. She kept an online cat diary for six months and each of her cats had about 50 online friends. "At that point, I thought, 'Who cares?' " she remembers. "Who cares if my cats have friends?" That's when she stopped writing about their adventures.[1]

So the question is one of engagement, which is all about content. How do you build relevant content that will get people coming, talking, returning to your site? How do you build the mix of user-generated and enterprise-generated content to do that?

Obviously, no one specific, concrete answer fits all situations. Companies and communities are far too diverse. The most I can do here is raise the issue and suggest some principles. I believe a good analogy is that of a brilliant magazine editor. The best editors understand their readers. They know what will interest, entertain, and excite their readers; what interests the readers of *Car & Driver* is different from, say, what interests the readers of *Skiing*. True, the two magazines' readership may overlap somewhat; some skiers are passionately interested in cars. But faithful readers would be surprised to find an article about a new ski resort in *Car & Driver* or a review of a new convertible in *Skiing*. Enough said.

Ten Rules for Private Communities

Sometimes your best bet is to set up a private, invitation-only community for your conversation. This is the specialty of Communispace, which creates consumer, customer, and employee communities that companies can use for marketing insights. Diane Hessan, Communispace's CEO, tells me that Communispace obsesses over how to keep community members returning regularly. Why? If members don't participate, the community has little value to the sponsoring company.

Following are 10 principles that Communispace has developed from its experience with private communities. While they apply most specifically to that firm's business model, they can be adapted to other communities, particularly in a business context. Any company with salespeople, distributors, dealers, franchisees, store managers, or other natural groups in far-flung places could profitably adapt these ideas:[2]

1. *Invite the right people, keep it private and small.* When you find people who have a common interest and put them together in a community, their energy explodes. Screen people to uncover interests, passions, and willingness to participate, and avoid using only simple demographic and geographic criteria. But keep the community private. More of the right people are likely to participate in private communities than in public communities because they feel more comfortable in an environment where they know what they say will only be seen by other identified community members, the facilitator, and company representatives.

2. *View members as advisors to the company.* Think of community members as valuable advisors to your company, not as a market research panel. When you treat community members as advisors they will go to amazing lengths to help your company—and for very little compensation. Despite high gas prices, people in one of Communispace's shoppers' communities drove over 100 miles to check out and compare competitive stores. An important note: Be sure to let your community advisors know how your company is using their ideas. The more you reciprocate, the more people will help you.

3. *Find the social glue, make it member-centric.* The more focused the community is on topics of shared interest and relevance to its members, the more involved they are likely to be. Don't base a community on just your product, service, or organization.

Rather, find the commonalities among potential members that are also relevant to your business, and ask people for help in better understanding that particular topic or domain. For example, rather than just testing drug ads, one pharmaceutical client is exploring the emotions behind a disease and how people make treatment decisions. A financial services client is exploring not just how people feel about their brand or even their category, but how and why members have come to consider themselves consumer activists.

4. *Work at building the community.* Communispace has found that, on average, 68 percent of community members are actively participating within 48 hours of joining. One reason for such high participation is that the firm creates community-building activities to help people understand quickly what the community is about, make them feel comfortable participating, and help them get to know one another over time. Some of these community building best practices are creating "rituals" like Tuesday night chats or "random thoughts" weekly polls asking people to post personal profiles, share personal stories relevant to the community's focus, or upload photos, like pictures of their favorite pet or the inside of their medicine cabinet.

5. *Be genuine, encourage candor.* The community's facilitator should set a genuine, open, and candid style and tone for the community. When a new member starts a conversation, make a big deal about how much you value the comment because this will reinforce the behavior. For example, "Hey, great idea. We want to hear everything so please say what you want." Or the reinforcement can be a spontaneous award. Make a conscious effort to give people permission to be honest and say what they really think.

6. *Just plain ask.* Companies often over-think how to phrase a question or issue to community members. The best way is to just ask in a simple, straightforward manner. One client company came up with a dozen ways to try to understand why

African Americans didn't use their products. Communispace suggested just asking African Americans flat out: "Why?" A retail client was worried about customers' reactions to store closings. The best advice: Post the press release and ask members what they have to say about the closings. Another successful technique is to ask members: "What are we missing? Is there something we didn't ask about that you wanted to share?" Members almost always say something useful.

7. *Pay even more attention to what members initiate.* While companies regularly poll members and ask them to take brief surveys and answer questions, the best insights often come from discussions started by members. How members talk to each other about how an issue or product "fits" into their lives can be incredibly revealing, as is how members influence one another. Within 24 hours of launching an investment community, for instance, 11 different dialogue topics were underway and only 4 of those had been seeded by the community facilitators. Members created the rest around issues they cared about. The lesson: Listen more than ask.

8. *Don't squelch the negative.* One of the most common mistakes marketers make is to try to squelch conversations about negative feedback. "We can't let them talk about that!" is a common reaction. However, some of the best lessons come from hearing about those things that annoy, disappoint, or outrage customers. Encourage members to give the good, the bad, and the ugly.

9. *Don't ask too much, too often.* As marketers get to know their community, many become overly enthusiastic about the ability to ask customers all the time, any time, about everything— new product ideas, advertising concepts, competitor moves. Don't ask members for too much too often or they will become fatigued.

10. *Use the right mix of technologies and methodologies, and keep experimenting.* Make sure the community is built on multiple underlying technologies and methodologies so that people aren't

stuck just answering surveys or posting to message boards, and so you can mine the insights with the right analytics. Engage members through a variety of functions: conduct live chats, create visual member profiles, use icons to classify discussion replies, upload advertisements; ask members to review products, keep diaries. Communispace recommends blending a range of methodologies and modes of expression including ethnographic, storytelling, mystery shopping, role-playing, video diaries, and polling. Similarly, keep experimenting with ways to more deeply involve people, create a richer community experience, and analyze what the community's conversations mean to marketing strategies.

"The primary reason that people don't belong to a community is because they don't think it will be worthwhile," says Diane Hessan. People don't usually leave a community they've joined, but their participation may drop. Software can track member participation, and when there's a drop-off, Communispace will send a note: "Hi, how are you doing? What is going on? We see that your participation has dropped."

Many of the reasons why participation drops have nothing to do with the value of the web site. Sometimes members get really busy, or a message may have been screened out by their spam filter, or they experienced technical problems getting into the site. "Given that our communities are pretty intimate," says Diane, "we have phoned participants to talk about this. If we think we have the right person and we are doing the right things, we want to know whether there is something we can learn for other communities. Can we do something differently to capture their imagination?"

What if someone doesn't respond and doesn't participate? "Because we have private communities," says Diane, "we control whether people are allowed in. If they are not participating, we replace them, because we have limited space. We don't take it personally. We just say this is somebody who is not interested and we are going to give somebody else that seat."

How Do You Pay for It All?

At some point, company management has to think about the expense of creating and maintaining a community. Where is the money going to come from to pay for this? I argue that a lot of this can be done inexpensively with existing web site templates, a digital camera, and a little imagination. Blendtec put its first videos on the web for less than $100. A small or local business—a restaurant, craft workshop, specialty toy store—can build a community around its content and include customer reviews and discussions. This lets visitors click into the conversation.

Larger companies may have to shift money from other budgets like television advertising—a movement that may already be underway. According to TNS Media Intelligence, in 2007 total television advertising spending dropped 1.7 percent (to $64.4 billion) from a year earlier while Internet advertising rose almost 16 percent (to $11.3 billion). Newspapers and radio advertising also dropped 5.6 percent and 3.6 percent respectively as consumer magazines, Sunday magazines, and outdoor spending rose. According to TNS figures, the Internet's share of measured advertising spending rose from 5.3 percent of the total in 2004 to 7.6 percent in 2007.[3] Taking a fraction of the national television advertising budget and devoting it to community building could have a far greater effect on the brand. Moreover, it could actually determine the effect because the social web is inherently measurable (as we'll see in Chapter 9).

Marketing on the social web will cost a large company far less and return far more than almost any other marketing activity. Paradoxically, you have to think like a really good television station of the past to be a really good purveyor on the social web. You have to be constantly thinking about content that will get people talking to one another and returning to your destination over and over. This is your opportunity to polish a reputation as a branded destination where visitors can have dialogues with other interested people. Go out to other people's parties, and also invite people back to your party. This is going to be an increasingly important shift in thinking as the social web expands.

Marketing budgets can be reduced and marketing departments can spend less time and effort in marketing to the social web. There's a bigger picture, too, if you look beyond the money angle. Earlier in this chapter, I mentioned that Stonyfield Farm embraced the environmental protection cause. How do you think its customers feel when they see the company investing to build a community and champion causes that could ultimately affect millions of people? Even if Stonyfield's causes aren't your causes, my point is that money can't buy that kind of brand reputation. So my last bit of advice about engaging communities in conversation is: Put your heart into it and think about the long term.

Step Five: Measure Involvement with New Tools, Techniques

(To Keep the Cutting Edge Sharp)

Throughout this book, I've argued that marketers must aggregate communities to reach and influence groups of people who share similar interests, concerns, or behaviors (or all three). But is it worth the time and expense? Research suggests that the answer is yes.

The Aberdeen Group recently compared the social media practices of 250 companies in various industries (heavy in high tech and publishing/media) and divided the firms into "best-in-class" (50 companies), "industry average" (125 companies), and "laggards" (75 companies). In several key areas, the best-in-class companies dramatically outperformed industry average.

For example, 94 percent of the best-in-class companies reported year-over-year improvement in customer satisfaction; the industry average was 49 percent while only 15 percent of the laggards reported improvement.

Also, 84 percent of the best-in-class companies reported year-over-year improvement in the number of actionable insights derived from social media monitoring and analysis. The industry average was 42 percent; the laggards, 11 percent.

While 84 percent of the best-in-class companies said they improved year-over-year performance in the ability to identify and reduce risk, only 37 percent of the industry average companies said they had done so—and only 4 percent of the laggards.

Finally, 86 percent of the best-in-class companies said they reduced the time between a marketing activity and delivering an analysis of the results to decision-makers. While more than half of the industry average companies, 55 percent, reported such improvement, only 19 percent of the laggards did.[1]

If customer satisfaction, actionable insights, identifying risk, and speedy analysis are important to a business, the Aberdeen report suggests that monitoring and analyzing the social web can be valuable. Fortunately, an entire industry has come into being to help you do just that.

On the Path to Payoff

Long before you start to measure the payoff—in fact, before you actually implement any social web initiative—you should clarify your objectives. You might aim for marketing objectives such as:

- Attracting new customers.
- Improving customer retention.
- Improving channel relationships.

- Building market share.
- Building brand awareness.
- Inducing product trial.

In addition, your financial objectives might include:

- Boosting sales revenue from specific goods and services.
- Improving marketing return on investment.

And you can certainly use marketing to the social web for societal objectives such as:

- Building awareness of and involvement in charitable or civic activities.
- Increasing awareness of specific issues (energy conservation, environmental protection, and the like).

Before you jump on to the social web, be clear about what you would like to accomplish . . . and what measure(s) you'll use to determine your progress toward reaching your objective(s). In fact, it's important to know *exactly* what you want to measure before you build whatever it is you're going to build. Remember, however, that your objectives and measures must take into account the *users'* experience, which is what communities are all about.

Suppose your firm wants to generate leads and your management says, "We need to measure conversion at each point in the user path." You want to know that someone entered the site and where he/she came from. I'll call this lead Larry (although, of course, you won't know names at this point). You want to know that Larry moved through the low barrier registration—gave a user name and picked a password . . . downloaded the case study in the site's low barrier area . . . submitted the additional information needed to gain admittance to the next tier, finally completed a form with his phone number or e-mail or more.

Larry likes to browse a lot, but you have to think through the value proposition. Is Larry really going to give his mother's maiden name for the honor of providing his e-mail address? This is a common blunder companies make. I know of one site where you must fill out a questionnaire just to download a case study that demonstrates the firm's capabilities. Sure, the firm is able to measure visitor movement every step along the way toward obtaining a lead, but it defeats another goal: to have as many visitors as possible download the company information.

Users will give you information to the extent they think they are getting something of value in return. This is why you can't lose sight of the user experience. Your company's gauge of value is not going to be the same as the users'. Senior executives may demand all kinds of conversion numbers before they fund a site, but at the end of the quarter they'll have only a handful of leads if they put up too many barriers.

The One-Two Punch

Once again, when you're considering measurement issues, don't forget what you already know. Online measurement challenges are similar to the kinds of challenges you'd face in direct marketing, advertising, and other types of marketing communications. If, for example, you're in marketing communications, how do you measure activity now? If you're an advertising manager, how do you measure ad impact today?

I'm well aware that we're operating in an era of accountability. Nowadays, chief financial officers want to know the return on the marketing investment just as they want to know the return on a new building or a new bulldozer. But do companies stop buying television time or print space because they can't measure, with real precision, the connection between the advertising and the sales? Obviously not. Instead, advertisers have settled on measurements, like gross rating points (GRPs) or cost per thousand (CPT), that relate to factors that syndicated research companies, like Nielsen, Arbitron, and MRI, *can* measure. Those measures enable TV networks, newspapers, and magazines to sell their advertising space in a way that feels fair enough for the advertisers who buy them. GRPs themselves have very little to do with measuring your marketing effort's effect.

This not to say you should stop buying traditional media. Depending on your product or service, your size, and your financial strength, you probably need to build some awareness, which you can do using various types of paid advertising. But not necessarily; you can now build it on the Web.

I see marketing on the social web as a one-two punch. One punch is the digital media marketing piece itself, in which you create content relevant to your marketing aims. These could be greater awareness, more inquiries, improved customer satisfaction, or the other marketing objectives you spelled out earlier. The second punch is inviting people to participate in, be informed by, or be entertained by that digital media experience.

It's All about the Data

E-tailers sweat bullets and spend millions on tracking software to make sure they know absolutely everything about the paths users take through their sites so they can optimize the browsing and buying experience. This is a little like (but much cheaper than) following customers through the store, observing the departments they visit, seeing which displays grab their attention, seeing where they spend the most time, and recording what they buy. If your company is not an e-tailer, you probably don't need to spend quite that much on Web analytics or spend so much time designing your site to trace a visitor's path. Still, you should look at certain things, depending on your objectives.

Table 9.1 lays out various metrics for media influence, audience, and business impact.

The easiest, and cheapest, to obtain are the media influences: visits/page views, unique visitors, and the rest. Google Analytics, Site Meter, Technorati, and other free tools offer a basic functionality to track discussions. You can be alerted when your brand or a keyword is mentioned.

For many companies, that's fine. If you don't have a lot of discussion around your brand, this may be all you need. But if you are a larger company, or if you are tracking a lively marketplace discussion, you will see the volume of activity overwhelm your ability to follow it through the free tools. Also, these give you no insight, no analysis.

TABLE 9.1   Success Metrics When Marketing to the Social Web

Influence on the Media	Influence on Your Target Audience	Influence on Your Business
• Visits/views • Unique visitors • Pages viewed • Volume of reviews, comments • Navigation paths • Links • Files embedded	• Sentiment of reviews, comments • Brand affinity • Commenter authority, influence • Time spent • Favorites, friends, fans • Viral forwards • Number of downloads • Opinions expressed • Membership	• Sales inquiries • New business • Customer satisfaction, loyalty • Marketing efficiency • Risk reduction
How compiled: Free tools: Google Analytics, Site Meter, Technorati, Yahoo! Search Management	**How Compiled:** Social media platform metrics Social media analysis tools	**How compiled:** Surveys Market mix modeling

You get the number of times your brand/company/name is mentioned and some other basic information.

At the other extreme are sophisticated tools like Cymfony (part of TNS, the giant research company) and BuzzMetrics (part of Nielsen). Jim Nail, the chief strategy and marketing officer for TNS Cymfony, points out that different touch points and information sources—traditional media, word-of-mouth, and much more—influence how consumers perceive brands or make purchase decisions. As traditional media has grown more fragmented and as the social web has grown, says Jim, both the number of influence points and the overlapping, intersecting ways these sources influence consumers in different combinations have grown exponentially more complex.

To help clients understand these influences on their customers, Cymfony uses a three-step process. "Step one is simply retrieving all of this stuff, and then de-spamming, de-duping, and all the rest necessary to get down to nice, clean, coherent, focused content relevant to that client," Jim explains. "Step two puts this through our natural language processing engine, dissecting paragraphs into sentences and sentences into parts of speech to understand what topics are being talked about. What adjectives modify the subjects of these sentences and paragraphs? Was the tone positive or negative and how was it changing over time?"

Step three begins to marry all this with advertising expenditure data and consumer behavior. "The more we bring together," says Jim, "the better a perspective we can give our clients on market influence and where they need to put their efforts to influence the target audience for their brand."

Listen, Engage, Measure

Somewhere on the continuum of purpose are tools like Cymfony and BuzzMetrics and tools offered by companies like Radian6, Biz360, Umbria, Visible Technologies, Coremetrics, Omniture, WebTrends, and several dozen others. Marcel Lebrun, the CEO of Radian6, says that tools like Radian6 are used for conversation tracking and are intended to be used by communications professionals (in-house or PR firms). The user is typically a communications expert who uses the information for outreach (blogger relations) or customer conversations. If executives have a research need or are looking for an analysis of opinion about a product or category, however, they will combine a service like BuzzMetrics with human analysis to produce a written report that adds a human interpretation to the data. For instance, a brand might employ BuzzMetrics to produce a report prior to and after a campaign to see what changed.

The Radian6 tool "integrates all of the online listening into one place, so it allows you to track automatically. It allows you to analyze the conversations to make sense of what is being said. And it helps you engage in a conversation to understand and measure certain things."

For example, say you have a well-known brand, says Marcel, and 3,500 conversations a day mention it. You want to understand which ones you should pay attention to first, so you need to measure things like the most engaged conversation. Which content are people spending the most with? "Or you might be interested in which conversation has the most influence," says Marcel, "and you might try to measure that." Once you've identified these conversations, you can decide to engage and track your engagement, either by introducing yourself, commenting, or following the conversations on Twitter, or on a social network.

You probably want to know whether people are saying good things or bad things about your brand. If you are Moosehead Beer, are people saying, "I like Moosehead"? When Moosehead sent beer to the Canadian troops in Afghanistan, that action provoked significant activity that could be measured by digital breadcrumbs: comments, unique commentators, social bookmarks, votes on social news sites, favorites on video sites, views on YouTube, and more. And all that's nice to know, but what good is it?

Marcel gives this example: Moosehead identified an article in which a customer said he was traveling on vacation to Western Canada and decided to try to buy some Moosehead (for a long time, beer could be sold only in provinces in which it was brewed). "Interestingly," wrote the customer, "the branding was different than I am used to at home, but whatever." Big disappointment. "I brought it home and the beer was terrible. What is Moosehead doing out here? They are destroying their brand. This product was sour."

Moosehead contacted the blogger and asked the store's location. He replied and the company investigated. They found they had an issue at the retail level; the customer had not bought genuine Moosehead Beer. They communicated that back to the blogger. The blogger then posted a second article saying he was amazed the company was listening.

Jim Nail at Cymfony says that one of the things that put the social web on the radar of marketers was the realization that people might be saying nasty things about the company and the brand. Companies didn't know what people were saying, how many were saying it, or whether to be worried about what was being said.

With a monitoring tool, you can classify what is positive and what is negative and then dig deeper. What are they saying that is negative?

Where is it coming from? How much negative conversation is going on? Is it starting to seep into more professional media company blogs? Is it starting to spread across the social networks? Does it jump to traditional media? "Things move really fast," says Jim. "If I can give my clients even a few days' notice, they can be much more prepared."

Imagine you're a toy company and news breaks of a recall because of lead paint. You would certainly like to know where people are placing the blame. If you have a portfolio of 20 toy brands, is one in particular taking all the flak? This is a good time to have your social web toolkit handy.

These tools can, of course, be used for positive guidance as well. An athletic shoe company wanted to find out why people buy one brand versus another. It analyzed the social media to establish what people were saying about each brand and which of each brand's attributes people liked and disliked. The company also analyzed the social media to determine which up-and-coming athletes seemed safest or smartest to use as spokespeople.

Evidence of and Quality of Community

The evidence and quality of the community is a somewhat qualitative measure, based on the premise that engaging your constituents, customers, partners, or prospects is a good thing. If you believe that having quality interaction with and between your customers is a good thing for thought leadership, for awareness, or for innovation—that it is a valuable activity—the case is made. If you don't believe this—or, more likely, you don't believe the effort is worth the return—you won't care about the evidence and quality of the community.

In many cases, a key goal of marketing to the social web is to learn, quickly, how your customers want you to improve your products and services. Assume that, in fact, you've set a marketing goal of generating new product enhancement ideas. You could build your community to encourage participants to generate ideas and then you'd count the ideas you actually get. For maximum accountability, measure from idea generation all the way through the product pipeline to see how many and which ideas are actually implemented—and how they fare with customers.

In other words, once the community becomes involved (especially when it's a public community), others are likely to say, "Hey, that's a terrific idea!" You do risk getting a reaction like, "Well, that's about the most ridiculous idea I've ever heard in my life." But I would argue that just getting a reaction is good—better than being ignored entirely.

You might have noticed that consumer opinion on the Web tends to split widely over books, movies, music, indeed, most products. "Both the customer you serve well and the customer you underserve have the loudest voices in the social media," says Sean O'Driscoll, general manager of community support services at Microsoft.[2] Look at the Amazon book reviews; they tend be written by people who absolutely loved the book (perhaps because they're related to the author) or who loathed it. Someone who is simply indifferent won't bother to say anything. It's people who have an interest one way or the other who are going to take the time and energy to voice their opinions— that's evidence of community.

It's Not All Milk and Cookies

Because the social web is inherently measurable, and because it's growing so rapidly, companies that offer Web analytics are also growing. As the demand for online measurement tools has grown, companies have responded.

Still, it's not all milk and cookies—there are real problems in what to measure, how to measure it, and what (if anything) the measurements mean. Brian Haven and Suresh Vittal of Forrester Research argue that marketing's new key metric is engagement—which consists of involvement, interaction, intimacy, and influence—and to measure engagement "marketers need to take four critical steps: define, audit, assess, and prioritize the metrics that are appropriate for their customer buying processes."

Haven and Vittal define *involvement* as the presence of a person at the various brand touchpoints. Metrics include "web site visitors, time spent per page, physical store visits, impressions from mass media, and advertising."

Interaction involves the actions people take while present at those touchpoints. Metrics include "click-throughs, online transactions, in-store purchases, and uploaded photos or videos."

Intimacy is the affection or aversion a person holds for a brand. Metrics include "sentiment measurement in blog posts, blog comments, discussion forums, customer service call sentiment, and the like."

Influence is the likelihood a person will advocate on behalf of the brand. Metrics include brand awareness, loyalty, affinity, repurchases, satisfaction ratings, forwarded content, and more. As Haven and Vittal point out, the metrics a company will employ vary by what marketing wants to accomplish. Creating awareness is different from driving transactions; building brand preference is different from increasing loyalty.[3]

In an ideal world, you'd like to be able to measure the social interfaces in relation to the number of actual transactions. For example, suppose you offer a podcast and a discussion with your customers about, say, accounting software. You include a Q&A session with the editor from *Accounting Today* as a guest speaker. You can now measure—EveryZing.com is one tool—the number of requests for information and product downloads. You can ask people how they found out about you before allowing them to download information or podcasts.

The content I've been talking about in this book creates an information circus. When you market to the social web, you have many things going on at once (professionally generated content, user-generated content, interactivity, everything else I've mentioned in earlier chapters). Does this circus of social interaction really have the payoff of pulling people through to try things or buy things? I believe it does.

For example, René Algesheimer, an assistant professor of marketing at the University of Zurich, and Paul M. Dholakia, an associate professor of management at Rice University's Jesse H. Jones Graduate School of Management, designed a year-long field experiment to find out. Collaborating with eBay Germany's managers, they identified 140,120 active eBay users, people who had bought or sold something on the site within the past three months but had not participated in eBay's online communities before.

Algesheimer and Dholakia randomly selected 79,242 customers and invited them via e-mail to participate in eBay's customer communities at the beginning of May 2005, offering them prizes such as iPods as an incentive to do so. The other 60,878 customers, who were not invited to join, served as the control group. So what happened?

"Within three months, 3,299 of the invitees became active community participants, posting messages, joining in discussions, and helping other members," the researchers report. "We call these customers the 'community enthusiasts.' An additional 11,242 users became 'lurkers,' reading others' posts without actively participating in the communities themselves." But what about their behavior?

The researchers say they were astonished at the differences between the two groups: "Lurkers and community enthusiasts bid twice as often as members of the control group, won up to 25 percent more auctions, and paid final prices that were as much as 24 percent higher, and spent up to 54 percent more money (in total)." Enthusiasts listed more items and their monthly sales were as much as six times higher than the control group's sales. Just as impressive, nearly ten times as many lurkers (56 percent) and enthusiasts (54 percent) started selling on eBay after they joined the customer communities.

For eBay itself, the increased activity of enthusiasts and lurkers "generated approximately 56 percent more in sales during the year that our experiment ran than in the previous year," Algesheimer and Dholakia observed. "With a take rate (the fraction of sales that eBay earns as revenue) of 10.3 percent and a gross margin of 82 percent, eBay earned several million dollars in profit from the increased trading behavior of the community participants in the experiment. Our results show that customer communities pay off handsomely for eBay and suggest that any online company will benefit from nurturing its communities."[4]

I'm a bit amazed that more blogs don't have what I would call a media kit. Increasingly, blogs have the tools to count and study their readers (remember, they know who their readers are) as well as to describe readers' characteristics. MediaBistro, for instance, offers a downloadable media kit describing readers by gender, marital status, age, income, education, and interaction with the site and its blogs. It tells prospective advertisers how many paid members the site has, how many registered users, and how many people are on the e-mail subscription list. It also provides opportunities for sponsoring events to target specific job titles, such as graphic artists, TV/broadcast professionals, editors, public relations professionals, and so on.

Because the paid media world has decades of experience in measuring and monetizing what works and what doesn't work in proceeding to transactions, it could help the social web world improve measures for marketers. Accountability is crucial: Companies want to validate that marketing to the social web is a powerful way to attract and engage a potential customer.

In Chapter 1, I mentioned Mini Cooper's use of social media to reignite buzz. The company sees a correlation between more online conversations, higher traffic on the Mini's sites, and more leads for Mini dealers. But is there a clear, direct, measurable connection between Mini's social web activities and the sale of cars? Mini would probably agree that the point is not to make an immediate sale but to get customers talking about the brand, feeling good about it, and thinking about it first when they're ready for new wheels. The sales payoff may be weeks, months, or years down the road. In the meantime, I suspect that Mini's paid advertising has been more cost-effective because the buzz increased brand awareness and laid the groundwork for building brand preference.

Step Six: Promote Your Community to the World

(Get 'Em Talking and Clicking)

B ecause there are a bazillion web sites on the Internet, how do you get people to visit yours? What if you invited a community and nobody came? Clearly, you have to promote your community just as you have to promote a new product or a new service. Compelling content is only the beginning. You have to use the social media to get people talking so they'll come to your community and get involved. Yes, you can use traditional advertising and direct marketing, but these efforts should be focused on sending people to your digital community to be informed, entertained, and heard.

Suppose, as an example, you were in charge of Aéropostale's marketing; how would you promote your community to the world? The principles of promoting your community apply to both consumer and business-to-business markets (and small and large businesses alike). Because you've probably seen Aéropostale's clothing stores in local malls all over the country, I'll use it to illustrate a few ideas.

What If: Aéropostale

First, a bit of background. Aéropostale's target market is 14- to 17-year-olds who buy fashion and active clothing and appreciate "compelling values." The company sells proprietary brands through its 800-plus mall stores and its web site.

If I were the head of Aéropostale's marketing and wanted to reach my market in a new, effective way, I would first identify the online communities in which my key constituents are active. Where do teenagers go online and what online activities do they participate in?

Let's say my research indicates that the young men I want to attract are into skateboarding and extreme sports. I know that the young women visit the various beauty magazine sites. How do I identify the bloggers who are talking about skateboarding and fashion (at the same time if not in the same place)?

I'll start by using the large search engines (Google, Yahoo!, Ask). This generates a list of the top industry news sites, blogs, and communities relevant to the domain. To produce a more extensive and targeted list, I use other searching tools (such as Brandpulse, Technorati, or Alexa), to find specific sites focusing on the individual keywords. Because the free tools are limited, however, increasingly people are using more sophisticated tools such as Cynfony, Visible Technologies, and Radian6 to do this.

Who is talking about Aéropostale the most online? I do that by simply typing words like, "Aéropostale," "Aéropostale jeans," and the like. In this way, I can identify sites and start to narrow the online community to the sites that talk about my brand the most.

Over the next month or so, I'll monitor these sites to see exactly what the bloggers are saying. I may find one was an anomaly; it mentioned the company once in a flurry of posts and never mentioned it again. Another blogger might write regularly about how she mixes and matches her Aéropostale clothes with accessories from other stores. Yet another might talk about where to find Aéropostale discount coupons online and when the store holds sales.

Now I know that blogger Susie Style is really focused on fashion and mixing-and-matching with other brands. I know that blogger Johnny Skateboarder is focused on cool T-shirts and shorts that make him look like an expert skateboarder even if he can't do a decent kickflip. With this knowledge, I can buy advertising in the community web sites for *Seventeen* and *Cosmogirl* which appeal to teenage gals who want to discuss fashion and related concerns. I can advertise on the Skateboard.com site or on the World Cup Skateboarding site to reach teenage guys.

Also, I can e-mail Susie Style: "I know you're writing about our clothes. I've been reading your blog. I like what you're saying and I want to get to know you. I notice you mix-and-matched our Aéropostale polo with an H&M skirt. Did you know that if you get a basic black polo you can use it 16 different ways?" I use my real name and let her know I'm from Aéropostale—this is not surreptitious.

Transparency is, in fact, a key point: You have to be open about who you are and what you want. Think of the social web world as a cocktail party. When you go to a party, you introduce yourself and often learn something about where the other person lives, what he or she does for a living, and what interests that person. You don't pull out a presentation and start flipping through the pages, no matter how attractive a business prospect that person might seem. You don't do that because you're in a social environment, and that's the way bloggers tend to think about what they're doing. A blog is a social conversation that people have with people.

My hope is that Susie Style will write in her blog something to the effect of: "You know what? I heard from this guy Larry at Aéropostale today, and he gave me a tip on wearing a black polo with this cute H&M skirt in a bunch of different ways." Johnny Skateboard might write, "I was contacted, and Larry who says he's from Aéropostale says I can get 10 percent off if I tell 10 friends to buy Aéropostale shorts. Each of us will get 10 percent off if we get 10 people to buy those shorts I was talking about last week." The blogging world may be social, but a company can still offer incentives to good customers.

Back in the real world, what do I say when Aéropostale's CFO asks me what all this will cost and how my marketing department plans to justify it?

I say this is a campaign. We're not going to write Susie Style and Johnnie Skateboard once and stop. It has to be an ongoing investment—but a relatively small investment for a large return. We've found that a company can spend as little as $2,500 to $15,000 to set up this kind of program; space in a national magazine can cost ten times as much.

And while my Aéropostale example is only that (the company is not a client and I have no inside knowledge of its operations), the company has already started marketing to the social web. Last year it teamed up with the teen charity Do Something to run a Teens for Jeans program. Any customer who brought in a pair of slightly worn jeans (any brand) got a 20 percent discount on his or her next purchase of jeans at Aéropostale. To jumpstart the donations, Aéropostale gave 10,000 pairs of its jeans to organizations that help homeless teens.

In addition to publicity in print media, both Aéropostale and Do Something promoted the program on their web sites. Lots of fashion blogs picked up on the program and YouTube carried a Teens for Jeans video with Rachel Bilson and Hayden Christensen. Even after the campaign ended, the Teens for Jeans page had the video available and linked to Aéropostale and Do Something to keep the dialogue going.

Now for a Real Example

For a real example of how to promote a community, consider ITtoolbox.com. This firm has created a growing community of information technology professionals since its founding in 1998. It now has 30 web sites with over 2 million pages of community-generated content that provides practical IT information and is supported by advertising. I recently asked Dan Morrison, the CEO and cofounder with George Krautzel, how ITtoolbox got started and how it's promoted.

First things first, Dan says: "Before you can even begin to market your community, you have to have something that users are actually going to find appealing, a value high enough to encourage them to participate. If you don't have that, you can promote as much as you want and you're still not going to get any participation."

The IT industry was (and is) an obvious candidate for such a community, if only because it's evolving so quickly. The idea for the site came when Dan, as an independent IT consultant, was working on a challenging tech issue with a colleague. Having exhausted their shared knowledge on the issue—and with no other place to turn—the colleague opened a book to search for the solution. Dan then realized that a site where IT professionals could share knowledge would be an extremely valuable resource and would be heavily used once professionals tried it and came to depend on it: "The value we were going to provide was that we were going to help a knowledge-based profession share that knowledge."

With that as a premise, they designed and put up the web site and began promoting it with the same tools they use today: word-of-mouth and search engine optimization. Once IT professionals tell their friends about the site, the friends tell *their* friends, and the word spreads. Search engine optimization (which I'll talk about in more detail in Chapter 12) is a good way to help people who are looking for the information you have. Both word-of-mouth and search engine optimization are extremely powerful in the community information model—far more powerful in the online community model than in the traditional editorial model.

"As a community, we view ourselves as competing with the traditional sources of information, which have all been editorial-based— primarily trade magazines and newspapers," says Dan. "In our case, the IT market historically has gotten all of its information through editorial processes, where a group of editors and writers create the information and then push it out to users in the publisher's chosen format."

While some communities on the social web are a mix of professional and member content, ITtoolbox users determine what topics they want to talk about and they create the content. That's the fundamental distinction between an online community and the traditional editorial model. And the online community model for an information web site, Dan points out, is very conducive to viral growth, word of mouth, and search engine optimization.

The Little Web Site and How It Grew

To show how to promote an online community, let me use ITtoolbox as an illustration.

Dan had been an IT professional; he'd worked at Ernst & Young and Deloitte, and had contacts in the industry. When ITtoolbox was launched in 1998, it was primarily a discussion forum for certain IT topics, along with links to relevant sources. Dan was excited to tell his contacts about this new service: "Guys, go check this out." They started using it, and very quickly Dan and George added some proprietary community tools to the forums. "We put it out and we got a little bit of usage, but we did something else," says Dan.

At the time, many people were using Yahoo! to find web sites. In fact, they were using the human-edited directory more than they were using the search engine. Even if they were searching Yahoo! they ended up searching the human-edited directory rather than what we think of today as a search engine index. "We got listed in Yahoo!" says Dan, "and we found ourselves listed in AltaVista and as soon as that happened, traffic spiked. We had up to five hundred visitors a day for some of the IT knowledge-sharing web sites. That was a really big spike. By getting that response, we were able to start building a critical mass of people who could then produce content."

What feeds search engines—and this is where communities are very, very good for the search engine model—is content, which communities generate in very high volumes. ITtoolbox is a phenomenal example of high volumes of very specific content that only gets more voluminous as community members answer questions and comment on the answers. That high volume of granular content is search engine food. The more you have, the more likely you are to show up in someone's search results.

A community like ITtoolbox, where the 1.3 million users create around 1,500 to 2,000 pages of content every day, has very granular content compared to the traditional media sources, which produce perhaps a few dozen pages of content per day. (And that would be for a fairly well-established media entity, because researching and writing is a timely and costly process.) At ITtoolbox, the thousands of community members have already done the research and are generating thousands of pages of content, day after day after day.

Another reason that communities fit so neatly into the search model is because of the evolution of search itself. Early on, people would search for a simple key term, then go to the web site and start checking out its content. Over time, they began searching using more complex key phrases. These days, people use search engines to search for a specific type or piece of information. As a result, having high volumes of very granular content is very conducive to drawing traffic to the community (in other words, promoting it). In fact, this search model is becoming the primary way that people use the Internet.

Searching brings new people into communities and as they become participants, they begin to create content—which leads to even more search engine fuel. It's a very synergistic model of people creating high volumes of content that is a very potent draw for search engine traffic.

Another key point: ITtoolbox is open to the public. Nonmembers can get into the site via Google, Yahoo!, Ask, or other search engines. But the community also has its own search engine, so that a member with a specific problem can search within the site. Dan and I believe that even a member-only site needs a mechanism by which members can search within the site.

Dan makes another important point about online communities: "If users can't find the exact information they are looking for, they can generally get the community to generate it for them by participating." What happens is that people tend to search and to find something, but that often generates another question or an extension of the original search. As soon as people want to interact with the community to get value, they should become members and provide information about themselves. What information they provide depends on the community sponsor's marketing goals and, as noted in the last chapter, may be nothing more than a user name and password.

Again, ITtoolbox's content is freely accessible. Yet the members' active participation adds value, because they are able to obtain information that is specific to their unique needs. They must become an active participant to request the community's help in acquiring that information—which builds the community and feeds successive rounds of positive word-of-mouth.

One Size Doesn't Fit All

Unlike a magazine or newspaper (or a television show or movie, for that matter), says Dan, it's challenging to build a prepackaged user experience in online communities. Remember, it's relatively easy for the traditional editorial media, which produce fewer pieces of highly researched content, to create a prepackaged user experience. In an online community, however, members are producing tons and tons of very specific content—and as the content gets more narrow and specific, the potential audience for each piece of content grows smaller—hypertargeted. Within a community, it's quite difficult to create a meaningful prepackaged experience around such hypertargeted content.

"This is one of the areas in which we're continually evolving," Dan notes. "Can we create some of our own prepackaged user experiences to introduce people to the content and help walk them through it to get to the right places?" ITtoolbox's answer was to create what it calls "knowledge bases," Each a focused web site that bundles all the community interaction related to a single IT topic. ITtoolbox has a web site for customer relationship management issues, for development and integration issues, for enterprise back office, for IT management and trends, and so forth. These serve as a sort of prepackaged user experience to showcase the type of content that the community is creating. They also provide a navigation path so visitors can find specific content. And, of course, they're one more way to promote the community to potential members.

In addition, ITtoolbox invites users to browse or contribute to blogs, wikis, and groups. It's got job listings, webcasts, e-newsletters, even a place to share vendor evaluations. Community members can choose the way they like to give or get information, dip in and out, or zoom in on a particular question they want to answer.

Now online communities like ITtoolbox can create a user experience built around individual members, a sometimes overlooked technique that's becoming more commonplace. "We introduced a social network into our community," explains Dan, "to allow users to create their own online profiles. Then they can link to others, similar to the concept of friends on MySpace. Because the goal of our network is to help people share information, we want to help members find people who have similar needs so they can exchange information. And as they share content, they're creating content that can be reused."

The social networking feature on ITtoolbox puts users at the center of the experience (and gives them another valuable benefit to mention to potential members). Here's how it works. Say that Alpha, a member, has identified 30 people with similar skill sets and with whom he wants to share information—and these people are all active participants in the community. If Alpha connects with those people on the profile page at ITtoolbox, he'll see all the content those people post. I'll talk more about this in Chapter 11, but you can already see how this feature would excite members and attract newcomers—promotion just by innovating for the community's benefit.

Outside Expertise

An entire industry of specialist companies has sprung up to help if you choose to go outside for expertise in promoting your community. Type "search engine optimization" into Google and you'll get more than 28 million results, with eight sponsored links (today, anyway). Google itself offers a wealth of free advice, but many consultants and agencies are ready to help. Interestingly, the company at the number 99 spot in my current Google search is PrairieWeb Internet Marketing, a Chicago firm that specializes in search engine optimization (SEO) and related services. A skeptic might wonder why there are 98 SEO results ahead of it. On the other hand, it's not at the number 1,000 spot.

By the way, the third link in my results list was to SEO Chat, which hosts tutorials, blogs, how-to forums, and similar tools and resources about the nitty-gritty of SEO. I'm sure more SEO sites will have this kind of social web component as time goes on.

Multimedia Outreach

Other ideas about promoting your community: This is where I would use some traditional media. Every print ad should include your URL. The Super Bowl ads increasingly point you to a digital destination. Traditional media can play a role by helping direct customers and prospective customers to digital environments.

Another obvious idea is posting your thoughts, comments, reactions, or all three on other blogs. Go to other people's parties to let them know you have some cool things back at your party that others might want to come visit.

You can always promote your web site the way companies have promoted themselves and their brands for years, with a contest. The social web, however, allows you even more options. For example, mainstream advertisers like Heinz, General Motors, and MasterCard have invited consumers to create and post their own commercials on the Web. Heinz has run user-generated commercial contests more than once, in fact. (You can see the latest winners on Heinz's TopThisTV.com site). Although Heinz's judges chose the finalists, site visitors voted on the winners. Heinz also included a "Send to a Friend" link to enable visitors to spread the word.

Millions of people viewed the videos submitted during Heinz's first contest. Millions of people also bought the product. Patrick Macedo, Heinz North America's ketchup brand manager, reported that year-over-year ketchup sales were 13 percent higher after that contest ended. No wonder Heinz launched a second contest less than a year later.[1]

Pepsi's Mountain Dew brand is doing a lot of multimedia outreach to engage its core audience of 18- to 24-year-old men. Although MountainDew.com is the hub, the brand reaches out through print and TV ads plus product packaging and in-store displays. Right now the star of the site is the Dew Report, a series of videos about non-mainstream sports like wakeskating and longboarding (you'll just have to view the videos to see what these are). Because Mountain Dew has long been associated with action sports, the Dew Report builds on that appeal.

The site also features music videos, online games, and game downloads to keep the most dedicated wakeskater at the keyboard for hours at a time. The site is fully equipped with the latest social web capabilities, such as the ability to Digg material, send content to friends, customize pages, and more. And it's a good draw, attracting about half a million unique visitors every month.

Mountain Dew is good at hooking into the wider world. In keeping with last year's election frenzy, it mounted Dewmocracy, a multimedia promotion that began with a massively multiplayer online game narrated by Oscar winner Forest Whitaker. As part of the game's storyline, players developed new Mountain Dew flavors. In the next stage of the promotion, Pepsi put the flavors to a web-based vote to choose three for test-marketing.

Now Mountain Dew offered Dewmocracy visitors a variety of tools to drum up votes for their favorite flavor. These tools included Facebook and MySpace applications, virtual bumper stickers and badges for blogs and web sites, favorite flavor message boards, and e-mail message templates. To encourage campaigning, the participant who recruited the most visitors to the Dewmocracy site was featured as Recruiter of the Week.

The election ended with Mountain Dew launching the winning flavor into the national market in November. More than 200,000 people registered to play the game and many thousands more voted for their favorites. When I did a Google search for Dewmocracy, I turned up results for press coverage as well as a number of blog posts. Clearly, Mountain Dew knows how to build brand buzz and involvement through social media.

Multimedia outreach is a great way to promote and build your community. For example, Kellogg's and its agency, Brigandi and Associates, rolled out an ongoing, integrated campaign for Special K cereal that combined television and print advertising, couponing, point-of-purchase displays, and a variety of social web tools. The target audience was women who want to manage their weight to look and feel great.

Marta Cyhan, vice president-worldwide promotions, noted: "We spend lots of time with women and clearly recognized that weight management is a journey." Kellogg's community (www.specialk.com), the focal point of the campaign, was designed to support women on this journey. The site, still up, offers weight management advice, describes Special K products, and invites visitors to share success stories, post messages, and ask for support e-mails by joining the Special K Challenge Yahoo! Group. In short, the site serves as a community for building relationships with and among customers.[2]

Kellogg's promoted the community through partners like *Shape* magazine; store displays and packaging that highlighted the challenge and the online community; print ads in parenting and fashion magazines; and commercials during TV shows with a large female audience. As Kellogg's Cyhan said: "Integration is the key to consumer engagement. The goal of promotion is to build the brand while motivating consumer interaction."

Best of all, the community has moved the needle on sales while attracting record numbers of new and return users. Sales of all Special K cereals registered significant growth during the campaign, blowing past the company's forecasts for existing and new products.

On the community side, page views were up five-fold and member registration doubled during challenge periods. Kellogg's community members are clearly engaged and find the site's content and tools so valuable that they return again and again—and tell their friends. Word-of-mouth has so much credibility that it can make (or break) a community. Combine that with multimedia outreach, and you can pack quite a promotional punch, as Kellogg's well knows.

Step Seven: Improve the Community's Benefits

(Don't Just Set It and Forget It)

Marketing to the social web is a journey, not a destination. It's a hike, not a camp out. It's a work in progress, not a statue cast in bronze. It's a . . . but you get the idea. You have to continuously improve the site and its value to the community. If you don't, you're liable to be MySpaced the way Friendster was.

What about Friendster?

Friendster wasn't the first social networking site. Back in the late 1990s, sites like Six Degrees and SocialNet came on the scene—and soon shut down. "We all basically hit the market before the market for social networking," says Reid Hoffman, the founding chief executive of SocialNet and the founder of the LinkedIn social networking site.

But by the time Friendster, founded by Silicon Valley engineer Jonathan Abrams, hit the Web, the market was ready. "Basically, Jonathan wanted to meet girls," Silicon Valley entrepreneur Mark J. Pincus told the *New York Times*. Pincus provided Abrams with some seed money to finance the project at the end of 2002: "He told me himself, he started Friendster as a way to surf through his friends' address books for good-looking girls."

Friendster was up and running in March 2003. Without spending any money on marketing, it attracted three million registered users within six months. The media jumped on the phenomenon: *Time*, *Esquire*, *Vanity Fair*, *Entertainment Weekly*, *U.S. Weekly*, *Spin*, and other publications wrote about Friendster; Abrams even appeared on the late-night television talk show "Jimmy Kimmel Live." (He then boasted that Yahoo!'s founders had never been guests on that kind of talk show.)

As Friendster's growth exploded and it attracted investors, it also attracted a board of directors, mainly experienced venture capitalists and software executives who had little feel for the product. The board assessed Friendster's situation and concluded that Abrams was in way over his head; in April 2004, he was replaced as chief executive.

What happened? "All of a sudden, Jonathan had all these high-powered investors to please," Russell L. Siegelman, a partner at the venture capital firm Kleiner Perkins Caufield & Byers, told the *Times*. "He had all this money in the bank, so there was all this pressure to hire people and get things done. Open up new territories: China, Japan, Germany. Add all these new features. Meantime, he took his eye off the ball."

The ball, of course, was the site and the user experience. As Friendster became more popular, the site became slower, eventually taking as long as 40 seconds to download—an eternity and a half for its 16- to 30-year-old target market. Yet, according to insiders, such technical difficulties did not interest the board of directors; they were more concerned with potential competitors and new features, such as trying to add Internet phone services to the site.

Kent Lindstrom, who became Friendster's fifth president in the fall of 2005, says, "The stars would never sit back and say, 'We really have to make this thing work.' They were talking about the next thing. Voice over Internet. Making Friendster work in different languages. Potential big advertising deals. Yet we didn't solve the first basic problem: our site didn't work." In retrospect, Lindstrom observes, the company needed to devote all of its resources to fixing its technological problems.

People inside the company realized they needed to add new features to the site if it was to compete with the newer social networking sites, such as MySpace, Facebook, and Bebo. "There really wasn't much to do [on Friendster] once you set up your network and found your old friends," says Larissa Le, a former Friendster employee. Other social networking sites were adding features like blogs and tools such as video that people could use to customize their profiles. But at that point, adding new features to Friendster would only slow it even more.

Another problem was that competitor MySpace allowed its users' personalities to come through, whereas Friendster, with a smiley-face logo, had focused on safety and trust. For the most part, MySpace lets its members do what they want. "The key to MySpace is that it's controlled by the user," says Joel Bartlett, an organizer for People for the Ethical Treatment of Animals. A few years ago, PETA was connected to both MySpace and Friendster; today, its site shows six social networking connections: MySpace, Twitter, Flickr, Helium, YouTube, and the organization's own issue discussion forums.

MySpace, founded in July 2003, boomed. By the end of 2006, MySpace had more than 50 times the number of monthly domestic visitors as Friendster, according to comScore Media Metrix. Meanwhile, Friendster's venture capitalists reconstructed the board and hired another chief of engineering, who focused on performance and stability issues until Friendster performed as well as other social networking sites. Friendster also announced an instant messaging service and began featuring videos from YouTube and other sources.[1]

Friendster now says it has 70 million users worldwide and is the top social networking site in Asia. It's also introduced a mobile site for cell phone users, available in several languages. MySpace remains way ahead of all other U.S. social networking sites, however. In Hitwise's research, Friendster didn't even make the top 10 list for the full year 2007 (while MySpace topped the list).[2]

Job One: Quality

Friendster's evolution has enough lessons for a marketing course (indeed, Mikolaj Jan Piskorski, an assistant professor at the Harvard Business School, uses the company as a case study in his strategy classes). The first real lesson is: *Maintain your quality*. In a sense, what happened to Friendster is no different from what can happen in a manufacturing environment when a product suddenly catches on and, in an effort to fill orders, the company cuts corners. Very simply, as quality declines, customers defect.

Remember, customers look at quality in terms of how well your site meets their needs, expectations, or requirements. Ensuring that every link leads to the right place and every image loads perfectly every time is just the price of admission. To give your community a heartbeat, you have to look beyond mere functionality. The real question is: Does your site give customers what they want today—and what can you do to anticipate and deliver what customers will want tomorrow?

You just can't introduce a product or service and leave it unchanged forever. Look at Coca-Cola, a brand that's been around for more than a hundred years. Coke is always introducing improvements like new flavors, different size bottles, and variations such as diet Coke and caffeine-free Coke. A web site requires the same kind of attention and constant improvement.

In fact, as soon as your web site goes live, it's time to start improving it. Review your goal for each section of the site. How are you measuring whether you've reached that goal? Is that a true measure of success? For instance, are you attracting a high number of visitors but no one is downloading your white paper?

What action would you like each visitor to take? Is it easy for visitors to find what they want on your site? Here, you need input from a sample of actual target customers, not your own employees or people from the agency that handles your account. Does your content/functionality make it easy for visitors to take action? You (or your web site designer) may think it's blindingly obvious that a red button labeled "Push Here to Download" means that a mouse click on the red button will initiate a download—but it may not be obvious to your visitors.

Every web site of any size should have a clearly marked site map so that visitors can see how things are organized. And think about the way you list categories. For example, a tab labeled "Press" implies that the content will be articles in outside publications, whereas a tab labeled "News Releases" implies content posted by your PR or marketing people. (Sites do confuse these two, as I've seen in my surfing.) In addition to a site map, you might also consider a search engine for the site itself, something you can buy right off the shelf from Google and others.

A Case in Point

A company called The Complete Website (tcwebsite.com) features case histories that suggest various ways to improve a web site. One of its cases focuses on six improvements designed to increase the number of e-newsletter subscribers for Andrea Novakowsky, a personal and executive coach.[3] Here they are:

1. Encourage visitors to your homepage to click the "Read the Latest Newsletter" or the "Read our Tip of the Week" button. Don't put the signup on the homepage. Web site visitors want to know what they're getting into before they give you their e-mail address. Be sure to position the e-mail subscription box close to the current newsletter. Also include text next to the newsletter or tip button that "sells/describes" the newsletter, white paper, or case studies you're offering.

2. Include a Tip of the Week page. TCWebsite says that after Andrea's homepage, this page is most popular.

3. Archive everything and provide an "Archives" link with the current newsletter. Archives increase your credibility.

4. If you have a testimonial or two about your newsletter, include it near your current newsletter, too.

5. Add a link to a Privacy Policy page so visitors can quickly and easily check your policy. For example, Andrea Novakowsky's Privacy Policy says, "We respect and are committed to protecting your privacy. We may collect personally identifiable information when you visit our site. We also automatically receive and record information on our server logs from your browser including your IP address, cookie information, and the page(s) you visited. Information Sharing and Disclosure: We will not sell your personally identifiable information to anyone."[4]

6. Add your signup form, a short newsletter description, and a link to the current newsletter on other subpages. No matter where visitors may navigate in your site, you should provide a quick way to find this type of content.

Peter Ericson, the president of The Complete Website, writes: "Think about the approach as relationship building." Let's say a visitor hears about your business and looks for you on the Web. That person starts formulating an opinion of your business as soon as he visits your homepage. Make that first impression a good one, and you're on your way to establishing the relationship.

Most visitors will be reluctant to give even an e-mail address without a peek inside your site. The thought process of a visitor clicking through your site, says Erickson, probably goes something like this: "Hmm . . . 'Read our Latest Newsletter.' Well, newsletters are great insights into businesses since they cover current activities . . . so I'll bite and click into the news. A quick read and oh, yes the newsletter is great stuff! I might subscribe . . . still cautious. A Privacy Policy . . . that helps. A testimonial on the usefulness of the newsletter—wow, people seem to love it. Archives . . . impressive . . . look at all this content! This is serious. Hmm well I'm a skeptic but, what the heck, I can always unsubscribe, right?"

Clearly, the system works only when the content you offer is actually useful to your target audience—and you have to keep on offering new and useful content—but then you know that by now. Enough said.

Gather Ideas

Another way to improve the community's benefits is to extend the web site's reach and impact. Here I want to focus on a few improvements made by Gather.com, a social networking site where members can connect with people who share their passions for books, food, gardening, health, money, music, politics, sports, travel, and more. Members can contribute thoughts, art, commentary, or inspiration and comment on other member contributions. One innovation involves a unique program with Amazon .com (a company that is itself a fascinating case history of constant testing and improvement). Amazon had introduced 49-cent Amazon Shorts, digitally downloadable short stories from published authors, both famous and unknown, who have titles available for sale through Amazon.com.

This improvement had unintended consequences that presented an opportunity for Gather.com. "Amazon's problem," Tom Gerace at Gather.com tells me, "was that it was turning away thousands of customers who were aspiring writers or very talented writers but who hadn't yet been published. As a result, these writers weren't eligible to participate in the Amazon Shorts program."

To address this situation, Gather implemented an improvement you can see at AmazonShorts.Gather.com. This is a writing contest, hosted on Gather.com, where unpublished writers compete to sell their short-form work on Amazon.com. Periodically, Gather members can submit short works (2,000–10,000 words) and compete for four spots in the Amazon Shorts program. Gather members vote to choose three winners and the Gather Editorial Team picks a fourth winner. Winners have their work digitally published and sold through Amazon Shorts, moving from the ranks of amateur writer into the ranks of published author in a matter of months. "It's one of the ways in which we create strong community identification," says Tom, "and bring a benefit to the community through aspirational programs like this one."

Another way that Gather improved its community's benefits was to ally with Nintendo to offer an area on Games.Gather.com where members can play and discuss games. Tom explains: "We identified the top six game writers on our site by the quality and popularity of their writing, then sent them Nintendo game sets with no obligation. We said,

'Look, we're going to have a sponsorship from Nintendo. We're sending this to you because you're a respected authority on games. Check out this set from Nintendo if you like, and if you want, review it, and if not, don't. But please be transparent if you do review it, and let people know we sent you the game set so everybody in the community knows we're dealing above board.' We were reaching out and saying, hey, we respect your opinion and we really want your thoughts on the product."

To help members navigate the site, Gather organizes content around nine categories (books, food, health, money, movies, music, news, politics, and travel). And it rewards participation through a point system in which active members can earn cash or gift cards for retail use or for charitable contributions. Click around the site, and you'll find "suggested groups" that include brands, such as the Starbucks Book Break and the Borders Book Club.

In planning improvements, your challenge is to dream up a game, a puzzle, an event, a cause, an issue that will make your site more valuable to visitors. Ideally the activity will connect to the brand, but not necessarily.

Gather gets the improvement process going by meeting with its agencies and partners to learn their strategic goals for the year. "We understand how they define their brand, who their target audiences are, how they're trying to reach those audiences, and what their key messages are," he says. "Then we work with them to develop 'wow' programs that benefit the community. We turn down programs we think will not create value, for two reasons. First, it will hurt the marketers and we don't want to create a bad experience for them. Second, it will hurt the community, and we're certainly not going to create a bad experience for our community. We'll only take programs that we think thousands of people will like." Final note: Gather invites visitors to join the conversation by suggesting improvements on improve.gather.com.

The Improvement Imperative

A tech community, in particular, can never stand still, as ITtoolbox's Dan Morrison well knows: "We've been around for ten years as an online community, so we've seen a lot of evolution—from the Web

1.0 days of community to Web 2.0. Because online communities are a relatively new phenomenon, a lot of innovation is going on and you have to be prepared to change and improve."

Even if you're not running a tech community, you must be sure that your central focus is always on providing value to a meaningful community. By "meaningful," I mean the community should be large enough to produce some kind of value for the members and for you as a business. At the same time, you should have the community as the center of your world and keep it there, building the community around members' desires, not around yours (or your boss's).

And you have to continually introduce innovative improvements to remain relevant to your community. At ITtoolbox, Dan has two pieces of advice on how to do this:

1. *Listen to your users and respond to them.* They'll tell you what they want. You can try to get them to do something, but ultimately members are going to do what they want and participate only when they find value. If you're an astute listener, you'll find clues to new features that you *and* your users think are valuable. No matter how good your site is, your users can always suggest improvements. If you respond to those ideas—to their desires rather than your own intentions—they will continue to grow the community for you.

2. *Be alert to new innovations and test them against the value you want to provide.* The whole idea of social networking wasn't even around—certainly wasn't very prevalent—just six years ago.[5] It started popping up and even then people weren't thinking about it in the professional sector. A savvy community operator constantly looks around for what's new and then thinks through the implications and possibilities.

Ask yourself constantly: What changes have occurred on the Web and in the industry, and how might those apply to me? Some changes may not seem relevant at first glance, but don't be too quick to dismiss something. For example, Dan remembers that when ITtoolbox launched a blog function in 2003, people viewed blogs mainly as opinionated personal journals. Blogging was a successful phenomenon in some parts of the social web for consumers, but would it translate well in the business-to-business world and provide quality content?

ITtoolbox persisted and dug deeper, Dan says: "Could a blog help IT professionals share information in a well-structured, predictable way? Yes, it could. If so, what would the program look like?" The company developed a structured blog program where members could (and did) post their daily experiences. A day in the life of a chief technology officer . . . a day in the life of a chief information officer . . . a day in the life of a security administrator. Suddenly ITtoolbox found members sharing very specific, very targeted information through a blogging platform, not something people were generally doing at the time.

Because ITtoolbox is all about helping people share information, blogging added value to the community. The blogging platform "has been very, very successful for us. We still have 300 percent year-to-year growth in our blogs program." Dan says.

The site also offers a social network feature that allows members to create their own online profiles and link to others, a la MySpace. How does this add value? Say a member identifies 30 active ITtoolbox participants with similar skill sets and with whom they would like to share information. The member connects with these people on his or her profile page and can then see all the content posted by the linked members. Not only can the member customize the profile and the experience, the chain grows as the linked members share information with still other members.

This improvement is extremely powerful because it puts users at the center of the community and allows them to build an experience around the people they choose to communicate and share information with. As users post new information, it appears on their profile pages and simultaneously on the profile pages of the members with whom they're connected. In a sense, this improvement is creating mini-communities as members connect with other members who are important to them.

Another important point: Adding a cool tool to your community may be fun, but it's not the tool that counts. If you don't give users the value they want, it doesn't matter whether you add a wiki, widget, blog, or the latest tech tool du jour. And Dan tells me that adding a single tool or feature may not be enough to deliver the value that a community expects or desires. Often you'll need a combination of tools, depending on the community, the average age of the members, and their interests and experience. So think about the value you're trying to provide and plan your improvements accordingly. If you have that mindset, it's a lot easier to continually innovate with the market (or maybe a little ahead of it).

Reality Check

You have an obligation to continually look for new innovations and figure out how they apply to your market—especially if you want to achieve or retain market leadership. If you don't, your site will become obsolete, more quickly than you'd expect because so much innovation is occurring in online communities right now.

After you've identified improvements you think will be valuable, you should get a reality check from your users by asking them: Here's what we're looking at, what do you think? How often have companies improved a product with features and benefits the market cares nothing about? (The answer: They do it all the time.) *You* may think the web site's new feature is wonderfully useful, but if your community doesn't agree, the improvement adds no value.

Let me share an example from the publishing industry. Not too long ago, John Lawn, the editor-in-chief of *Food Management* magazine, announced that his publication wanted to provide a better search capability to help readers find posted articles online. He also asked readers to give some direct feedback on the topics and search functionality they'd like to see on the site. Although not a complete cookbook for user feedback, here's a sample of his questions:

- What kind of content from past issues of the magazine do you consider it important or useful to be able to access?
- What a kind of content that hasn't appeared in the magazine would you like to see in our online presence?

- What topics or categories of information would help you the most?

- Can you give an example of something you'd like to look for on our site, but can't easily locate now?

- What bothers you most about the way our site's information is right now?

When I asked John about reader response to the column, he told me it was disappointing. "Most of the time people don't take the time to respond that much any more. They are just too busy. If you really hit a nerve you might get a dozen responses." Nevertheless, his experience has suggested ways to learn what people *do* want: "Start one-on-one interviews to find out what basic user needs are (sample users from different job positions, responsibility levels). Probe to find out what gets in the way of satisfying them. Create simplified lookup systems with answers to common problems and good indexing to technical resources. Create an easy-to-browse (and interesting-to-browse) mechanism for general-purpose communication. And write 'FYI' ticklers that provide very short 'lead-ins' to information on less common problems."

John, who earlier in his career worked as a communications manager in a large corporate data center, argues that web site designers and editors have to understand their users' needs and find ways to satisfy them by making key information and content readily accessible. "Very often, technical people who are very skilled in the mechanics of web or software design (but who aren't very experienced at creating user content) are charged with making the information accessible, and they do it poorly," he says. "In many large companies, web site design and maintenance often gets centralized within technical groups that tend to focus on standardizing maintenance and technical support to satisfy internal system needs and efficiencies, rather than by focusing on the users. In contrast, Apple has always done a pretty good job. So has Ernst & Young, which has always focused on 'Knowledge Management' strategies." Two sites to check out for ideas.

My last few words on the subject (and I can't say it too often): As technology and markets evolve, you can't simply create a site and leave it unchanged. If you don't regularly improve the community's benefits on terms that make sense to the members, your site could fade away. Remember Friendster: At its low point, it still had millions of members, but most of them had not visited the site for more than a year.

You may not need (or want) more and more visitors, but you do want your members to come back often. The best way to bring them back is to constantly add new and different features or pages, add tools or information that make the site more useful, more interesting, more fun, or all three.

Making Use of the Four Online Conduit Strategies

The Reputation Aggregator Strategy

(We're Number One!)

W hat, you ask, is a reputation aggregator? A site that provides rankings of content/sites. (I discussed reputation aggregators briefly in Chapter 7, in the context of online conduit strategies). Reputation aggregators are a key—perhaps the key—gateway for most users to reach online content. People use these sites to decide what content they want or need when they're getting ready to buy, researching schools, looking up statistics, and so forth. The most heavily-used reputation aggregators, ranked in order of total searches by a recent Nielsen Online report,[1] are: Google, Yahoo!, MSN/Windows Live, AOL Search, Ask.com, My Web, Comcast Search, AT&T Worldnet Search, NexTag Search, and Dogpile.com Search.

I call these sites reputation aggregators because, if you're going to search for anything, search engines like these aggregate the findings. They put sites or results or products in some kind of order—the most recommended or most linked or most used or bestselling or most visited, for instance. Because people can't buy your products or digest your ideas if they can't find you, you have to understand how search works and how it seems to be evolving.

Everybody Loves Search

According to a Pew Internet & American Life Project study, search engines are decidedly popular among Internet users. As the study's author, Deborah Fallows, wrote: "Searching the Internet is one of the earliest activities people try when they first start using the Internet, and most users quickly feel comfortable with the act of searching." Take a look at some of the study's findings:

- 84 percent of Internet users have used search engines, and on any given day, 56 percent of those online use search engines.
- 92 percent of those who use search engines say they are confident about their searching abilities; more than half, 52 percent, say they're "very confident."
- 87 percent of searchers say they have successful search experiences most of the time, including some 17 percent of users who say they always find the information for which they are looking.
- 68 percent of users say that search engines are a fair and unbiased source of information; however, 19 percent say they don't place that much trust in search engines.

Fallows noted that while people have positive feelings toward search engines, few are highly committed to searching. Most (67 percent) say they could return to the traditional ways of finding information. About one third of the search engine users search every day, but most search infrequently; almost half say they search no more than a few times a week. Nearly all (93 percent) settle into the habit of using one or two search engines.

Now here's a particularly important point to bear in mind. Fallows found that while most consumers understand the difference between a regular television program and an infomercial, or between a magazine article and an advertorial, "only a little more than a third of search engine users are aware of the analogous sets of content commonly presented by search engines, the paid or sponsored results and the unpaid or 'organic' results." In fact, only about one in six searchers said they could consistently distinguish between paid and organic results.

"This finding is particularly ironic," she wrote, "since nearly half of all users say they would stop using search engines if they thought the engines were not being clear about how they present their paid results. Users do not object in principle to the idea that search engines will include paid results, but they would like them to be upfront and clear about the practice of presenting paid results."[2]

What Am I Bid for "Laptop"?

As the readers of this book know (even if two-thirds of the Americans who use search engines do not), paid search is where companies either bid on key words, or—growing more common—rent a word for a certain period. If you type in "laptop" on a major search engine, you're likely to see a number of "sponsored results" on the results screen. Google, Yahoo!, and Ask all have a list of advertisers running down the right side of the results page. A recent list included Microsoft, Gateway, CircuitCity, and Shopping.HP.com. These search engines also head their results pages with several sponsored links set off from the rest of the results. During my laptop search, I saw Dell and BestBuy at the top of the first results page.

In general, companies have a financial interest in being out in front where people can find them immediately. Why? Two reasons. First, my Google search for "laptop" turned up 275,000,000 results— an unimaginably large list of results to wade through. Second, research shows that most people do not go more than three screens deep into a search. So if you are Lenovo, trying to reinforce brand recognition after the Beijing Summer Olympics, it may be worth bidding high to be number one in Google's listings. You don't pay anything unless a searcher actually clicks on the link, and presumably the only reason people click is because they're shopping for a laptop. What do you have to lose?

On the other hand, there have been cases of click fraud, where unprincipled companies click repeatedly on a sponsored link to drive up a competitor's advertising expense. The search engines say they're aware of the problem and they're dealing with it, but you should also know about this issue when you think about search.

A recent study commissioned by Google—which clearly has a vested interest in paid search—quantified the rewards for brands that top both organic and paid search results.[3] If your brand leads both the paid listings *and* the organic listings, the study showed that recall is 220 percent higher than if your brand has neither a paid ad at the side nor a top spot in organic search results. Many marketers believe it's important to have a presence in paid and organic results, in part because different consumers have different search strategies. I'll get back to that point in a moment.

But does your brand or company really have to be number one in the result listings? There is, after all, a huge difference between someone who clicks through to your site and someone who actually buys your product. Every store has more browsers than buyers. You may do almost as well in terms of actual sales by being second or third or lower in the sponsored sites. Certainly you'll pay less for your ads than the company in the top spot.

Indeed, "bidding the highest amount for a keyword to ensure that your company tops the list of results may be a path to campaign failure," says Timothy Daly, senior vice president at SendTec, a St. Petersburg, Florida-based direct marketing services agency. "Recent research by San Francisco-based eye-tracking analysis software firm EyeTools, combined with what we see day in and day out with our clients, leads us to the conclusion that being number one in most cases is a waste of money, while camping out in a lower position often proves to be more productive."

Daly says that his agency commonly encounters a CEO or a vice president communicating downward to the search manager that "we want to be in the number-one position at all cost." And it goes the other way; the search manager wants to impress superiors and bids for the top spot without any regard for the relationship between cost and effect. Yet the number-one spot is not always the best place to be.

"When two or three companies all have the 'top position' mentality," says Daly, "they almost always start a bidding war with each other, constantly raising bids until the top two or three bids are way out of tune with what's economically viable. Budgets are burned. Results are poor. And eventually, these bidders fall back to earth or disappear."[4]

Web Marketing Today Free Weekly says that organic search is more visible on the page; paid search is less visible except for the ads above organic search results. The full results of organic search may take several months to show up, whereas paid search's results take only several days. That means it can be difficult for your firm to obtain a top position in an organic search's results listing; it's usually fairly easy, however, to buy the top position in the sponsored results if you're willing to pay the price. Also traffic for organic search depends on the position for various key words, which can vary by search engine; in paid search, traffic can be high for all the important key words.[5]

Remember that simply posting fresh content automatically moves your site up in the organic search ranks. When you don't keep improving your site with fresh content, you sink in the results because other people are coming in with new stuff. New content signals to the search technology that a site has something not seen before by search users. (Want more ideas about improving your ranking in the results? Search for "search engine optimization" and follow the links to the advice, agencies, and consultants that show up.)

Of course, if your brand lands high enough in the organic search results, you may not need paid search. Or you can follow the advice of Justin Yates, sales director of the U.K. SEO company Just Search. He recommends buying lower-cost niche key terms and optimizing your site to land higher in search results for the key terms that are out of your price range.[6]

And be sure to integrate your reputation aggregator strategy with your other marketing activities. Here's what happened when Marks & Spencer, the U.K. retailer, launched a multimedia campaign to build awareness of its car insurance offerings and drive traffic to the M&S site. In addition to TV commercials, outdoor advertising, and direct marketing, M&S's search-engine strategy included paid-search on generic key words ("car insurance") and on branded terms ("M&S car insurance").

Three months in, M&S fine-tuned its online approach. After evaluating the performance of its paid-search words, the company cut its budget for the high-cost generic terms and boosted its budget for the branded terms. The result: slightly lower traffic to its site but a 74 percent drop in the cost of new customer acquisition. In fact, M&S says its investment in search engine marketing was 99 percent more cost-effective than its investment in traditional media activities.[7]

Ready for Landing

The importance of search is growing because we're flooded with information and searchers want answers quickly. Search and the social web are going to be an even more important pairing in the future, because users will want to search, but also want validation from other people. They'll want to hear the opinions and thoughts of other people who've used that product, had that experience, taken that cruise, bought that laptop. Users will want to leave questions for other users or at least read posted comments because these seem more credible than the company's advertising or public relations.

This is why you must understand how your customers are using search to find you. For instance, after Kodak took a close look at how buyers search for industrial printing equipment, it redesigned its site. Kodak's goals were "making sure [buyers] are presented with information appropriately and logically, and making it easy for them to contact us and become a lead in our system," according to Brian Nizinsky, a marketing manager in Kodak's Graphic Communications Group.

Although you need to know the proper key words to guide buyers to the right page on your site, don't forget that Marketing 101 still applies. Kodak's Nizinsky says to "optimize the page for the user, not for the key word."[8] In fact, an entire specialty has grown up around the process of optimizing landing pages (the first page a visitor lands on when clicking to your site). SiteTuners.com, one of these specialty firms, tests everything from headlines and page layout to color, buttons, forms, and navigation. Get people to the landing page with the information they need, when they need it, and watch your conversion rates rise.

No wonder engineers are always looking for ways to improve search. I'd like to spend the rest of this chapter talking about some of the current activities. I'm listing them in the sure knowledge that by the time you read this there will be more announcements—and it's possible that some of these search engines will have been bought, folded, or changed direction.

Don't Ask Jeeves, Just Ask

I see Ask.com as a microcosm of the kind of change that's taking place in search engines. It began life as AskJeeves.com, promising users they could use ordinary English to search, for example: "Who has a good value in laptops?" Unfortunately, that didn't work particularly well, and when the dot-com bubble popped, Ask Jeeves almost popped with it. By 2005, the Jeeves name was history but today the site is going strong, thanks to its ongoing search innovations.

Instead of ranking results based on the number of links a site has to other web sites, Ask first clusters sites based on content categories, then chooses the most popular sites in those categories. The idea is to spike the results with specialized sites that are the most authoritative on a given subject, even though these sites may not be the most popular.

Another innovation is AskCity, a service that integrates maps with information about local businesses, restaurants, concert and movie listings, and reviews. If you search for a Japanese restaurant in New York City, for instance, you see a listing of restaurants by neighborhood together with a map pinpointing the locations. You can search by a specific neighborhood or for another kind of cuisine. Directions are available with a click; you can text-message the restaurant listing to a cell phone with another click. It's easy to check out individual restaurant reviews through Citysearch or make reservations through a service called OpenTable.

Users can also select one restaurant and then search for nearby movies, concerts, or other events, and then book tickets for those events right on the site. AskCity will display (or e-mail or text) walking or driving directions from the restaurant to the movie theater or concert hall. For local marketers—restaurants, movie theaters, entertainment venues—the site can be a good way to reach prospective customers when these people are most interested in a meal and a show.

This should give Ask a competitive edge since local searches already account for 10 percent of all Internet queries and are expected to grow faster than other searches.

Ask.com also differentiates itself by giving users previews of the web sites that appear in search results and offering simple ways to narrow or expand the results. In a search for the keywords "California and wine," for instance, a set of options will appear next to the results, allowing users to focus their search on, say, California wineries, wine regions, wine prices. It's easy to then expand a query to find Napa wineries, southern California vineyards, or famous foods in California.[9]

NexTag is a comparison shopping site for products, financial services, travel, automobiles, real estate, education, and more. The search engine enables shoppers to compare prices and find the best deals on millions of products and services.

Dogpile is a metasearch engine that taps six search engines to find what you ask. As their site states, "different search engines often return different search results for the same query. Based on everything from how information is arranged on a web page, to what each search engine pinpoints as most relevant, search results can vary widely across each search provider." The site's "technology removes duplicates and analyzes the results to ensure the best results are always on top of the pile."

Beyond Plain Vanilla Search

What I see coming in reputation aggregators combines scalability of existing search engines with new and improved relevancy models. Search sites are bringing in user preferences, collaboration, collective intelligence, a rich user experience, and other specialized capabilities that make information more *productive*. The following, with no pretense of being comprehensive (there are at least 100 specialized search engines as I write), is a selection of relatively new approaches to give you a flavor of how the field is changing. Two caveats to keep in mind: The information about these search engines comes mainly from their web sites, and I'm not endorsing any one of them. They're here as a service, not as a plug.

EveryZing is an audio and video search engine and online advertising network. Using speech recognition technology, EveryZing searches words within both audio and video, not just the metadata, to classify content based on topic and usage. EveryZing helps consumers find audio and video content based on keyword searches and then allows them to browse the results for relevance, just as text results can be browsed. Consumers can jump to a specific location in the audio and video without fast forwarding or listening to the entire file. On the business side, EveryZing offers marketers online multimedia playback ads tied to consumers' specific search terms and categories. This helps advertisers link directly to the growing volume of video and audio content that consumers go searching for.

Endeca was designed to help people find, analyze, and understand information on individual web sites. For example, suppose a consumer visits HomeDepot.com—an Endeca client—and type "drills" in the search box. Search will come back with categories of drills and prices so the user can tailor the search and get more relevant, specific results. This, says Endeca, enables organizations to increase revenue, decrease costs, and streamline operations by helping their customers, employees, and partners find answers to questions quickly and easily. Retailers, manufacturers, distributors, publishers, government agencies, financial services firms, healthcare organizations, hospitality businesses, and professional service providers would find this valuable.

ChoiceStream allows people to personalize the content they receive online, on television, or on a mobile device. No more looking for programs by TV station; instead, users type in "Lost" or some other program name and they can actually watch the program. The search engine becomes the channel aggregator and the television networks just become content providers. Karen Leever, senior vice president of Directv.com, says: "We chose ChoiceStream because it learns from customer interactions quickly and accurately to understand their unique preferences resulting in a relevant recommendation system that delivers enormous value." For marketers, ChoiceStream is a way to target, connect, and communicate with consumers.

Clusty got its start in Pittsburgh in 2004 when the search software company Vivísimo brought its technology to the Web. But the story really starts in 2000, when Vivísimo was founded by three Carnegie Mellon University scientists tackling the problem of information overload in Web search. Rather than focusing just on search engine result ranking, says cofounder and CEO Raul Valdes-Perez, "we realized that grouping results into topics, or 'clustering,' made for better search and discovery. We're trying to move search away from this idea that ranking Web pages is the solution to everything. Instead, our basic philosophy is, don't just try to show the best ten or the best five pages, but instead dredge up a larger amount of stuff, the top 200 or 500, organize that quickly—in half a second or so, and show the major themes to the user."[10]

Clusty queries several top search engines, combines the results, and generates an ordered list based on comparative ranking. This meta-search approach helps raise the best results to the top but instead of delivering millions of search results in one long list, the search engine groups similar results together into clusters. The clusters not only save users from having to scroll from page to page, they cover results that might have been missed or buried deep in the ranked list. Clusty can also be used to search shopping information, yellow pages data, news, blog posts, and images.

More Flavors of Search

Swicki, like Endeca, is a search tool that an organization can add to its site. Its purpose is to learn and adapt automatically, based on the community's search behavior. Swicki ranks results (including videos) based on the actions taken by the people who search a site, because there's usually some level of commonality between users of any given site. According to the Swicki site, "With every search, vote, and click, your Swicki generates more relevant results and turns into a valuable asset for you and your community." Eurekster created Swicki to improve users' search experience, allow web sites of all sizes to host search, and enhance search engine marketing for advertisers.

Rollyo and Swicki pursue a similar goal: community powered, theme-based search. Rollyo enables users to create and publish their own personal search engines, based on web sites they decide to include in their "Searchroll," Rollyo's name for such a personal engine. With Rollyo, searchers can create personal search engines using only the sources they trust (news articles, blogs, etc.). It requires no programming, and the company offers a starter kit of Searchrolls a user can personalize.

Lexxe, based in Australia, has been developing a new generation search engine with advanced natural language processing technologies—similar to the original Ask Jeeves idea. According to the company, "Lexxe has been exploring more intelligent ways to find information for users in a more meaningful way. We believe this method will eventually bring far more accurate and relevant search results than the current search technology."

Wink is a people search engine, pure and simple. If you want to find an individual who's part of a social networking site somewhere out there, this is the search tool to use. You can narrow your search by location, interests, groups, even distance. The results pages are organized according to the social networking site(s) where this person is listed plus a set of Google results focused on the name you searched. If you want to be found quickly and easily, join Wink and write your own Wink profile.

Gravee is another meta-search engine, which means it combines the results of many different search engines into a single set of results which are further refined by the company's technology. As Gravee users click to "vote" on the relevance of any of the individual results in their searches, the search technology takes those votes into account when displaying future results. Gravee also allows users to add tags (additional keywords describing content) to search results and bookmark their favorite web sites with notes and descriptions.

Gravee shares advertising revenue with content owners and compensates them for making search results possible. When a user clicks a keyword search ad on Gravee.com, up to 70 percent of the ad revenue generated is divided between the ten sites whose content is included in the organic search results on that page. To clarify, that is 70 percent divided by 10, or 7 percent of ad revenue to each web site on the organic search results page for every ad clicked.

ZoomInfo offers concise Web summaries with social networking aspects. ZoomInfo, which calls itself a summarization search engine, finds, analyzes, and extracts information from web sites, online press releases, electronic news services, and SEC filings. The results are summarized in a comprehensive yet easy-to-read format.

eMvoy is an interesting entry in business-to-business search. It is for suppliers of plastics and sheet metal, industrial fabrication, machinery and tools, raw materials and chemicals, and services such as testing, assembly, prototyping, and engineering. To make the search results more valuable to the manufacturers who use it, eMvoy rates suppliers on 24 quality, reliability, and stability factors.

All of these should give you a taste of where reputation aggregators are today and where they may go tomorrow. In the future, search will continue further down two paths: contextual and social search. Contextual search is where you know the context in which you want to search: MySpace, Gather, YouTube, even retail sites like Amazon, Sears, and Ikea.

Social search is where you are asking other people for their experiences: Have you been to St. Kitts? What's your experience with KitchenAid? Can you recommend a good Italian restaurant in St. Louis? Search is already so important to the social web that you *must* have a strategy for getting into the results for users who matter for you—and for leading new community members to your site.

The Blog Strategy

(Everybody's Talking at Me)

By the time you read this, the blogosphere will have expanded well beyond 112 million blogs. That's right, 112 million blogs—some personal, some professional, all adding their voices to the social web.

A typical blog combines text, images, and links to other blogs, Web pages, and other media related to its topic. The vast majority are primarily text, although some focus on photographs (photoblog), audio (podcasting—more about this later in the chapter), or video (vlog or vodcasting, more later) and are part of a wider network of social media. Microblogs such as Twitter, also discussed later in this chapter, are increasingly popular.

Blogs are hardly new. Online diaries and journals began appearing in 1994, and the term *weblog* was coined by Jorn Barger in December 1997. The short form, *blog*, showed up in 1999 and quickly became both a noun and a verb, what the thing is as well as what you do when you're doing it.[1]

Now there are so many blogs that special search tools like Technorati and Google Blog Search have sprung up. In fact, since Technorati was founded in 2003 by David Sifry, it has tracked the growth of blogs. According to Technorati, the number of blogs has doubled about every six months. Every day, more than 100,000 new blogs are created and 1.3 million new posts are added to existing blogs. Meanwhile, tens of thousands of blogs sit frozen in time, with no new entries, and thousands more are simply abandoned as people move on to something else (Twitter or YouTube or whatever).

A survey by communications expert Paul Gillin, of Framingham, Massachusetts, found that bloggers are active readers of other people's blogs:[2]

- 96 percent of the respondents say they regularly read one or more blogs.
- More than 41 percent of respondents read more than 50 blogs a week.
- More than 25 percent read more than 100 blogs a week.

Bloggers are also skeptical of marketing. A survey by Edelman public relations focused on how bloggers interact with business. Asked to rate the trustworthiness of various business sources on a 1-to-10 scale, respondents assigned an average value of 4.6 to a message from a public relations firm. Messages that come directly from a company did somewhat better, at 5.5 out of 10.

When Edelman asked, "When looking for product information, which do you trust most?" almost 63 percent of the blogger respondents cited "other bloggers;" only 31 percent noted company web sites or press releases. The results confirm the assumption that bloggers are a community bound together by trust. This affinity creates an environment in which one blogger is able to influence many others, leading to vigorous discussion and the occasional swarm.[3]

Speaking of trust, last year's Edelman Trust Barometer noted that 25- to 34-year-olds find Wikipedia (the free user-written online encyclopedia) the second-most credible source of information about a company; the most credible source is business magazines. Wikipedia finished way ahead of all kinds of media news, all company communications, and the company's web site. Dead last on the list of credible sources: corporate or product advertising. Even blogs, YouTube, and MySpace/Facebook (in that order) were more credible sources of company information than corporate or product advertising.[4]

Blogs Go Big-Time

In the blogosphere, the self-edited and the authoritative tend to rise to the top. Don't make the mistake of assuming that blogs are bloated with half-baked ideas and crackpot opinions. It is a myth that people who spend time on these blogs and boards and social networks and things are complete whackos, says Jim Nail at TNS Cymfony. "Maybe that was the case fifteen years ago when it was all about user groups and a lot of it was very techy, geeky people and academics in their narrow specialized disciplines conversing with each other. But it has not been the case for a long time."

Look at your favorite study, says Jim—Forrester, Pew, Jupiter, eMarketer, whatever—and look at the percentages of people who are engaged in social media activities. "These are not entirely mainstream people, true. But they are not the radical fringe at the extreme end of the bell curve, either. Since we joined up with TNS, a big traditional market research company, we have been doing a number of projects to look at what we find opinions to be in social media and what our colleagues find to be in traditional research. You are dealing with different methodologies and different sample groups, so there are bound to be some differences, but directionally by and large they are generally the same."

Maybe blogs aren't the New York Times or the Los Angeles Times, the New Yorker, or PBS. Certainly among the millions of bloggers, a wealth of half-baked crackpots regularly belch their opinions. But readers are quick to point out mistakes. And if the mistakes continue, all but an unreconstructed hard core committed to the source will fall away.

A recent *BusinessWeek* article pointed out that ordinary bloggers have a lot of competition these days from *megablogs* with paid staff members. Blogs like TechCrunch and GigaOm, for instance, have the resources to ferret out hot stories that are critical to their readers. Using Technorati, *BusinessWeek* found that nearly 171,000 sites link to the TechCrunch blog, a must-read for Silicon Valley insiders and dealmakers. "That's more than (gulp) Businessweek.com," the story concluded.[5] Gulp, indeed.

In fact, I see a new generation of media authority developing rapidly in the blogosphere. I believe the blogosphere is mirroring the evolution of newspapers only in a New York minute. It took decades for the *New York Times*, *Le Monde*, or the *Financial Times* to become brands, but the Diggs of the blog world are becoming trusted information partners to a new generation. They're being held accountable for accuracy by readers rather than by editors and fact-checkers. Blogs will not entirely replace newspapers, but I predict that in five years, no American newspaper will have more than a million (hard copy) readers. Increasingly, consumers and businesspeople will look to blogs for specific, timely, expert information and advice.

Half the news destinations right now are blogs, says Technorati, including the *New York Times*, MSNBC, CNN, the *Washington Post*, the BBC, *USA Today*, NHK, and the *San Francisco Chronicle* among many others. There is a maturation process in the blogosphere that is going to continue with increased sharing of social media; more and more we'll see "mainstream" media saying, "Slate said . . ." or "Medpundit said . . ." or "WebMD said . . ." or "The Huffington Post said . . ." or "The Drudge Report said . . ."

And, as the blogosphere evolves, bloggers are going to be more professional; they're going to look for more resources. More than a third of the respondents to the Edelman bloggers-and-business survey said they blog to gain visibility as an authority. (What kind of an authority is often wrong?) In Paul Gillin's survey, one-third of the respondents listed "career advancement" as motivation for blogging, "perhaps reflecting the large number of consultant bloggers." Overwhelmingly, Gillin says, people noted intangible factors as being more important, factors like connecting with others, influencing markets, and 'it just feels good.'" So watch for the blogosphere to become equal to—if not heavier in weight than—traditional media within the near future.

So Why Get Blogging?

I talked to Elisa Camahort Page, one of the co-founders (with Lisa Stone and Jory Des Jardins) of BlogHer about reasons why business-people might blog. Like everything in business, it depends on your goals. Perhaps the first reason, says Elisa, "is to establish thought leadership. Particularly if you are a small or start-up company, having a blog is a way for an executive in the firm to talk about the industry, to talk about the market space, to establish credibility, to get some search engine juice going. All this helps not only with customers, it helps with media and PR efforts because reporters and writers are trolling the blogs all the time for people to quote and interview and cite. They use blogs as a reference now. For an executive who wants to raise her profile—and therefore up the company's profile—a blog is a great way to help secure speaking engagements, contributed articles, and quotes in major media. All of that adds credibility, which eventually can trickle down and make customers, who may be used to buying other brands, products, or services, feel more comfortable with you."

Conversely, a blog can help humanize a large company that has a broad customer base. Elisa notes that Microsoft's hiring Robert Scoble as their blog evangelist and encouraging their developers to blog to put a human face on the corporation. It made people more comfortable interacting with them, and more comfortable being that customer. When Bob Lutz, the head of General Motors' North American operations, started blogging, he started getting hundreds of comments from people who wanted to talk to GM but never had anyone to talk to. "Now they see this guy," says Elisa "He's a senior executive, he's blogging, they let you comment. He responds to comments and suddenly it is an entirely different interaction with a company that was previously just a monolithic faceless entity."

The third reason an executive might want to blog is to escape the echo chamber and get a feel for what is taking place in the field. When a company is small, Elisa observes, most executives are in tune with their customers. "But as you grow and build your team, you get more and more removed. A blog, if nothing else, is a direct line to your customers. They can comment; they can give you feedback. They can tell you what they want—and you have the ability to respond, which is really the fourth big positive. People are on the Internet talking about you anyway."

This is a key point: You can't control your message. You never really could entirely, because you could not control the back fence discussion, the kitchen table conversation. But today, people not only are having these conversations you can't control, they're public. "The concept of controlling your messaging is obsolete," says Elisa. "It's delusional almost to think you have control. But, if you create a space online where people can come to have a conversation with you, and you participate by responding—whether on your own blog or by commenting on other people's blogs—you have the ability to become part of that conversation, which you certainly never did when someone talked about you at her kitchen table."

With all this in mind, start with the practical issues you confront every day. You can search the blogosphere for the best plastic to use in a certain manufacturing process, the best distribution network, the best reseller, the best whatever. Virtually anything you're looking for, you'll find discussed and dissected by experts who are blogging.

Autoblog's experts, for instance, "obsessively" cover the auto industry. Engadget is "a web magazine with obsessive daily coverage of everything new in gadgets and consumer electronics." (Notice the obsession with, well, being obsessive?) TMZ is "your official site for the latest entertainment news, celebrity gossip, Hollywood rumors, celebrity video and photo galleries." BlogHer's mission is to create opportunities for women who blog to pursue exposure, education, community, and economic empowerment. All heavy-weight blogs with a lot to say and a lot of people who check in—obsessively—when they're online.

Get Your People Blogging

The commercial side of the web is moving from a transactional model—go to a site, buy something, leave—to the social web model—go to a site like a blog, see what people are saying, leave a comment, check out links to other sites, leave a comment, compare user experiences, buy something, comment on the experience, and leave. Josh Scribner, technical project manager and architect in IBM's corporate communications, says that Big Blue is looking hard at this new model.

Josh tells me, "We've been promoting blogs very heavily for the last year and a half. We have some of our executives talking from their own perspective, but at the same time they're talking about topics that are important to the industry. They're talking to investors; they're talking to their business peers; they're talking to CIOs and CTOs and folks like that. This is extremely important because it shows leadership for our brand. Sharing expertise to show leadership is the kind of strategy that any firm can use."

Another Big Blue example comes from Ed Brill, business unit executive, Worldwide Lotus Notes/Domino Sales, IBM Software Group. Brill has been building a community of Lotus software users through his blog (www.edbrill.com) since late 2002 and, more recently, Twitter postings. "I found naturally that the people I could get to read the site were my customers, and there was an extended sense of community in my customers. The product we work with is collaborative, and the blog kind of became my way to reach that audience," says Brill. "I found that the one-to-one community interactions became incredibly powerful for decision-making in my own job and for feedback in my own organization. It also keeps me up on competitive trends."[6]

IBM is so supportive of blogging that its site has a page listing company bloggers and what they blog about. To avoid misunderstandings, the page carries this disclaimer: "As they'll tell you themselves, the opinions and interests expressed on IBMers' blogs are their own and don't necessarily represent this company's positions, strategies or views. But that doesn't mean we don't want you to read them! Because they do represent lots of business and technology expertise you can't get from anyone else."[7]

Without a doubt, the best-known corporate blogger is Jonathan Schwartz, the CEO of Sun Microsystems. He says: "My No. 1 priority isn't spending time communicating; it's ensuring that my communications are broadly received. Blogging to me has become the most efficient form of communication. When I blog, I'm talking to the world. I can write a blog in an hour and a half and share something substantive with everyone. But for me to get to Sao Paulo for a meeting with Brazilian customers is easily a two-day operation."

Schwartz notes that about 10 percent of Sun's employees—including the corporate counsel—currently blog, an activity he definitely encourages. "One of the wonderful things about blogs is that I don't have to walk through the campus to figure out what's on people's minds. I just go to blogs.sun.com and I read what they're thinking. It is a daily visit for me."[8]

For Schwartz, blogging reveals the authentic voice of the organization. It is "living the brand." Insincere or phony blogs will not fool anyone for very long—remember the Wal-Mart blunder. Schwartz also believes, as I do, that blogging is an effective and inexpensive way to market the company and its products. "The thing to understand about blogging, and the thing to understand about the Internet as well, is that silence is rarely your friend," says Schwartz. "In a vacuum, somebody else will be speaking on your behalf about your company, about your brands, about your executives or about your employees."

Schwartz told a British reporter he once had an argument with a customer who wanted to know, "Why on earth do you write a blog; it has no impact on me or on the marketplace?" Schwartz's answer: "Well, maybe not on you specifically. But if I'm writing a blog and you're reading it, a journalist is reading it, an analyst is reading it, or an investor is reading it—they're not reading something else. They're not reading what my competition has to say. At a certain point, everyone is in competition for your attention. Everyone is in competition for being able to sell you something, being able to appeal to you as a consumer. Advertisers are in competition for your affinity. Employers are in competition for your attention. I want you to pay attention to Sun. The network is a more efficient way of doing that, better than expensive PR."[9]

Not surprisingly, blogging has caught on in political circles, not simply as a campaign device but as a way of engaging constituents. Bob Lynn, a member of the Alaska House of Representatives, has blogged since his election in 2002. Although his blog covers legislative matters, "it also includes my personal take on current events and issues, and it allows people to get to know me better as a person." Colorado House Speaker Andrew Romanoff found that after he began blogging, he got much more input from constituents.[10] Sounds like a good way to know what constituents—otherwise known as customers—want, think, like, and don't like.

You Do Want to Hear the Bad News

But isn't there a danger in allowing just anybody inside and outside the company to say anything in public? What about competitive information? Trade secrets? Proprietary data? After all, loose lips sink ships.

Yes, there's a danger. So for comments coming from outside the company, I agree that it's both legitimate and prudent to establish a process for screening out the irrelevancies, obscenities, and liabilities.

Every responsible senior executive wants to hear the bad news, whether it's a negative reaction to a new policy or a customer gripe that could be an early sign of something far worse. The problem, says Jonathan Schwartz, is the natural tendency to keep bad news away from the boss. He says that Scott McNealy, Sun's chairman and former CEO, told him, "Always worry about what people aren't telling you."

Nick Jacobs, CEO of Windber Medical Center in Pennsylvania, doesn't hesitate to blog about controversial issues or even bad news. I read one post in which he discussed—at length—a critical letter he received concerning lapses in patient care. "As a patient-centered hospital that has reached some degree of recognition nationally, this letter represented not an A in patient centered care, but very close to a C, or worse," Jacobs wrote.

After explaining what the medical center has done to improve, he added: "In closing, this is not a blog that is intended to demean, take unfair shots, or berate our staff, it is meant to say that transparency is exactly that: transparent." No wonder this CEO's blog (which includes YouTube videos of the medical center's latest doings) draws hundreds of thousands of readers, people in the industry plus immediate stakeholders and prospective staff members.[11]

That said, however, you can't have it both ways. You can't invite outsiders to comment on company products, policies, and performance and allow only the enthusiastic or innocuous to be heard. These days, word will get out faster than you can imagine, and the firm's timidity will be exposed. I believe it's far better to take your lumps and correct the problem. As Josh Scribner at IBM says, you want to head off problems or be able to address them. "IBM has been making a great effort to keep an eye on what's going on out there and listen to what our customers have to say."

What about bloggers within the company? How can you confidently allow employees to blog?

When I have this discussion with senior executives, I can only respond with these questions: Do you trust your employees? Do they cheat on their expense accounts? Steal company supplies? Freelance during company hours? If there's no trust between employees and managers, if managers believe that most employees are basically dishonest and looking for a way to rip off the organization, then allowing employees to blog about the company is probably a bad idea. (Obviously, the company cannot stop an employee from blogging about, say, her gardening challenges, when she's at her home computer and on her own time.)

If, however, senior management believes that most employees are basically honest, the issue is one of guidelines rather than control. Josh says that when IBM decided to go into blogs in a big way, management carefully considered the issues and established guidelines for employee bloggers. These guidelines included "things like: don't get into an argument with people, because there's no point. Be the first to apologize. Say who you are. We want people to say who they are and to say that their opinions are not necessarily those of IBM."

Still, Josh knows that companies worry about what might happen if an employee blogger says something wrong or inflammatory or otherwise inappropriate. What then? "You need to make sure that it is clearly explained that they are talking on their own behalf, because that will satisfy a company's legal team. That's how we work with our own legal team here."

IBM also insists on transparency, meaning employees must say they work for IBM if they blog about IBM. This is critical, Josh emphasizes, because readers should "feel we're being honest when we're out there. We don't have subterfuge in the blogging world."

Rules for Employees Who Blog

Let me go back to Sun for a moment because it's so active in encouraging employees to blog. Browsing the "About Sun" section of its web site, I found that the company posts employee blogging guidelines with this introduction: "Many of us at Sun are doing work that could change the world. We need to do a better job of telling the world. As of now, you are encouraged to tell the world about your work, without asking permission first (but please do read and follow the advice in this note)." Because these guidelines are so apt and well-written, I want to include some here (picked up almost verbatim from Sun's site):

- *It's a two-way street.* The real goal isn't to get everyone at the company blogging, it's to become part of the industry conversation. . . . If you start writing, remember the Web is all about links; when you see something interesting and relevant, link to it; you'll be doing your readers a service, and you'll also generate links back to you; a win-win.

- *Don't tell secrets.* Common sense at work here; it's perfectly okay to talk about your work and have a dialog with the community, but it's not okay to publish the recipe for one of our secret sauces.

- *Be interesting.* Writing is hard work. There's no point doing it if people don't read it. Fortunately, if you're writing about a product that a lot of people are using, or are waiting for, and you know what you're talking about, you're probably going to be interesting. And because of the magic of hyperlinking and the Web, if you're interesting, you're going to be popular, at least among the people who understand your specialty.

   Another way to be interesting is to expose your personality; almost all of the successful bloggers write about themselves, about families or movies or books or games; or they post pictures. People like to know what kind of a person is writing what they're reading. Once again, balance is called for; a blog is a public place and you should try to avoid embarrassing your readers or the company.

- *Write what you know.* The best way to be interesting, stay out of trouble, and have fun is to write about what you know.

- *Financial rules.* There are all sorts of laws about what we can and can't say, business-wise. Talking about revenue, future product ship dates, road maps, or our share price is apt to get you, or the company, or both, into legal trouble.

- *Quality matters.* Use a spell-checker. If you're not design-oriented, ask someone who is whether your blog looks decent, and take their advice on how to improve it. You don't have to be a great or even a good writer to succeed at this, but you do have to make an effort to be clear, complete, and concise. Of course, "complete" and "concise" are to some degree in conflict; that's just the way life is. There are very few first drafts that can't be shortened, and usually improved in the process.

- *Think about consequences.* The worst thing that can happen is that one of our sales reps is in a meeting with a hot prospect, and someone on the customer's side pulls out a print-out of your blog and says "This person at your company says that product sucks." In general, "XXX sucks" is not only risky but unsubtle. Once again, it's all about judgment: Using your blog to trash or embarrass the company, our customers, or your coworkers, is not only dangerous but stupid.[12]

Blog or Tweet?

Once you decide to blog, post often. The posts can be short—indeed, shorter is usually better—and they should be entertaining. Your blog should be connected to and engaged with the blogging community in your arena. Get to know the other people who write on your subject and engage with them.

Remember that blogging takes an enormous amount of commitment and dedication. Make time to read blogs related to your field, understand who's blogging and why, and actively participate in the conversation. Also think carefully about what might happen if your words provoke the community and how you might want to respond in such a situation. Speed counts. If you travel frequently and can't check your blog on a regular basis, you might not want to blog at all.

Elisa Camahort Page at BlogHer says that companies typically make a big mistake when telling an employee who already has a 100 percent job to add blogging. "They haven't really thought about allocating their resources. A blog is a program, and you need to allocate resources just like you would for any other program that was a marketing program or communications program or a customer care program. The same thing goes for the executive's time. What is he/she not going to be doing to accommodate this in her schedule?"

Consider a group company blog using managers or employees throughout the organization, which has the added bonus of giving readers a sense of all the different teams under one roof. Occasional blog posts from members of the executive team are great, so don't set the expectation that the blog is only written by one person all the time, much less the CEO. The exception to this rule is a CEO who really wants to be the voice of the company, really knows how to write and *really* understands the time commitment that blogging requires.

The CEO can write occasionally, when the situation demands it. But so could people from the manufacturing group, from sales and marketing, from finance, from human resources, from every function. You can either make your group company blog public and available to outsiders for comment or keep it private, strictly for internal bloggers and readers. That's a major decision.

If something happens in your business at 11:12 A.M., you can blog about it at 11:13 A.M. If someone disses you or says your company has committed an error, a crime, or a bad deed, you can react instantly. That's the beauty of blogging.

Marketers should also be aware that advertising has arrived in the blogosphere. A number of blog hosting platforms and software companies have programs that permit a marketer to post ads within the posts. If someone writes a blog on plastics and you're a plastics manufacturer, that's the place for you.

Of course, you want to know that someone is reading the blog. In fact, before you buy an ad, you'll want to know as much as possible about the blog's audience. Who it reaches, where they live, demographics, psychographics, behavior, and more. I encourage marketers to do a deep dive to analyze the top tier blogs, the ones most important to their communities.

Now a quick word about blog spam. Some businesses are using automated means to post content and links disguised as comments on blogs. If you want customers to trust you, don't use blog spam, don't hire agencies to spam blogs, and remove these kinds of comments if you find your company or employee blogs have been spammed.

Another warning: Don't even think about putting up a flog (fake blog, also known as a flack blog). You've probably seen some legitimate-looking blogs that talk up products (such as new movies) without any hint of a corporate connection. When such flogs are unmasked—and they always are—the blogosphere goes wild with outrage over being misled. If that's not enough to give you pause, consider that fake blogging for marketing purposes has been outlawed in the United Kingdom. When in doubt, be transparent.

Finally, if you want to know what people are saying about your company or product in the here and now, check out Twitter. It's a microblogging tool that limits messages ("tweets") to 140 characters or less. Don't just listen—post your own tweets to keep the conversation going. Dell, for instance, datamines tweets for product mentions and then mobilizes employees to respond. The CEO and employees of Zappos, an online clothing retailer, regularly post tweets about what they're doing and use Twitter to answer customer inquiries. Think of Twitter as a short, snappy, and speedy social networking tool.

Now Listen up! Podcasting Is Here (Vodcasting Too)

A podcast is a media file that creators—companies or individuals—distribute by subscription (paid or unpaid) over the Internet using syndication feeds, for playback on mobile devices and personal computers.

A vodcast is video on demand—like a podcast but with video. More about that later.

Though podcasters' web sites may offer direct download or streaming of their content, a podcast is distinguished from other digital audio formats because you can download it automatically using software capable of reading feed formats. A bit of trivia: Podcasting was named the word of the year by the editors of the *New Oxford American Dictionary* in 2005. The word provoked some controversy because it seems to imply that an Apple iPod is needed to listen to podcasts, when in fact all portable media players (and most newer PCs and laptops) will play them.

Initially, podcasting's appeal was that individuals could distribute their own "radio shows." It didn't take long for the system to be adapted to a wide variety of other uses, including distribution of school lessons, official and unofficial audio tours of museums, conference meeting alerts and updates, and public safety messages.

Podcasting is an increasingly popular communication tool for staying in touch with customers and other important audiences. Sun Microsystems offers at least a dozen podcasts on its web site, including a "news" podcast about the latest from Sun and interviews with various Sun engineers and executives. Its vodcast series, Level Up, is all about the latest developments in videogame technology.

Then there's Sun's Virtually Everywhere Podcast, which "allows you to listen to Sun innovators, customers and partners discuss your top IT and business pain points and find out how Sun software and solutions can help you solve them."[13] Think how valuable it would be to have your customers talking about their problems and then listening to how your company can solve these "pain points." That's the power of podcasting.

UNICEF, the charity, offers numerous vodcast downloads to spread the word about issues, problem areas, activities, and accomplishments. Carrefour, the French retailer, offers both podcast and vodcast downloads of its latest news releases. NASA even uses vodcasts to give people an inside look (literally) at the space program. What can vodcasting do for your organization?

You can't afford to sit back while competitors jump on the blog, podcast, or vodcast bandwagon. Blogging is not just a fad. "The data shows this is where your customers are going," says Elisa Camahort Page, "and they are stealing time from other places you used to reach them—newspapers, magazines, TV, radio. When people are asked how they get the time to spend all the time in the blogosphere, they get it by spending less time doing these other things. You need to worry about it because that is where you will find your customers. Most companies want to talk to their customers in some way. If you are not reaching them on the blogosphere, there is some percentage of them you are not reaching at all." If you want to be seen as a market leader, if you want to reinforce your ties to customers, if you want to shape the conversation, go out and make a place for yourself on the social web right now.

The E-Community Strategy

(Go to Their Party or Throw Your Own)

If the blogosphere holds millions of blogs, the Web has hundreds of thousands of e-communities. Back in Chapter 7, in the discussion of building your own community, I defined e-communities as sites where people aggregate around a common interest and often includes professional content. Whether the common interest is business or personal, people join these communities and return to them regularly because they offer news, information, entertainment, or all three. In this chapter, I want to talk about how you can connect with somebody else's e-community or build your own e-community to reach the people who matter to your business.

Thousands of e-communities are already drawing sizable audiences, with new sites being established daily. The pioneer—and prototypical—e-community was Slate, which Microsoft founded in 1996. Michael Kinsley, Slate's founding editor, says that for the first few years it was referred to as "Slate, Microsoft's experimental online magazine that some people read on their computer via the Internet...." Today they say, "Slate reported yesterday...."[1] Slate, now owned by the *Washington Post*, is no longer an e-community but has evolved into The Slate Group, an online publishing unit with several specialized news and opinion sites for targeted audiences.

By my definition, the main Slate site has a number of e-communities: news and politics, arts and life, business and technology, health and science, style and shopping, travel and food, and sports. These are communities not only because of the common interests that members share, but because Slate's visitors can comment on and discuss the articles posted by the professional writers and reporters.

By the way, you may remember that Slate once charged a subscription fee, but not now. These days it relies only on ad revenues, which means the content must be good enough to attract and retain a sizable audience over time—no small consideration for an e-community.

Inside the Parenting E-Communities

Lately I've noticed a lot of e-community activity around the topic of parenting. There's Babble, which Nerve Media launched in 2006 as "the first parenting magazine designed from the ground up for a new generation of parents—mothers and fathers who increasingly share the work of raising children, live in cities, and use the Internet to access information." BabyCenter and CafeMom are focused on parenting, and iVillage has pages devoted to conversations among mothers, as well.

All this activity is hardly surprising, considering the size of the market. According to U.S. Census data, some 82 million women are mothers, and 4 million women give birth every year. Also men, a big target readership of sites like Babble, are more attentive to their children than previous generations. A University of Maryland study, "Changing Rhythms of American Family Life," found that married fathers spent 6.5 hours a week on child care in 2000, up from 2.6 hours in 1965.

However, as the *New York Times* has noted, newsstands and library archives are filled with current and departed parenting magazines, and today's Web is full of mommy and daddy blogs, message boards like UrbanBaby.com and social networking sites like Maya's Mom (mayasmom.com, "Where parents share") and MothersClick.com ("Connecting. Learning. Sharing"). What does this mean for Babble?

Julia Beck, founder of 40 Weeks, a consultancy serving the expectant- and new-parent market, said, "This is a new generation of parents who are interested in taking their existing lifestyle, sense of self and priorities into parenting, as opposed to checking them at the parenthood door. They're looking for ways to infuse their personality and aesthetic into this new phase of life, and all this new lifestyle parenting media reflects that."[2]

Babble and all the other parenting sites will have to do what magazine publishers have long had to do: attract an audience—or an e-community—for advertisers that want to reach those people. They'll have to convince media buyers that they actually have an audience and that the audience has characteristics important to the advertiser. That's where you get your opportunity to go to somebody else's party, mingle with visitors, and maybe invite them to a party of your own.

Remember that you can augment your e-community strategy through specialized social networking sites that attract your desired audience. Let me stay with the parenting topic for a moment. If you're in Indiana, the *Indianapolis Star*'s IndyMoms.com is a local site for parenting discussions and questions; if you're in Boston, you might click on the *Boston Globe*'s BoMoms.com site. Then there's Meetup.com, which hosts a number of local parenting groups that coordinate get-togethers among participants. All are social networking sites, not e-communities, but they offer companies opportunities to get into the conversation in different ways.

Here's an example. Kimberly-Clark, maker of Huggies and other brands of baby products, is a heavy user of traditional media but it's also jumped into social media with branded e-communities like huggiesbabynetwork.com. In addition, Huggies has joined the social networking party with a pilot program of sponsoring 100 local Meetup parenting groups.

"We started with feedback from Meetup members and organizers as to whether they would want a sponsor and what they would find of value from a sponsor," says Brad Santeler, Kimberly-Clark's director for media and relationship marketing. "It's very transparent. We asked them what they wanted, and we're providing that." No stealth marketing here—everybody knows about the sponsorship angle. And it has real value to participants, because the company pays the monthly fees that these groups would ordinarily pay to Meetup.

Kimberly-Clark sees these Meetup groups as natural places for brand discussions to develop. According to Kate Johnson, the company's consumer relationship marketing manager, "When you have one mom talking to another, it's powerful. So we're offering them information and tools and activities; we're not in their face with advertising."[3]

Electrons Beat Paper and Ink

An online e-community like Slate or Babble has a number of advantages for both publishers and readers that a paper-and-ink publication does not have, however, including:

1. It pays nothing for printing, binding, and postage. (It does pay for bandwidth, but generally nowhere near as much.)

2. The site contains moving images and sound as well as text and color photos.

3. Information can be timely; there's no gap between writing a story and publishing it.

4. An online publication can link to other sites on the web; one click and a reader jumps to a source, a company report, an earlier article, or something else that adds to the current article's depth and richness.

5. An online publication accumulates an archive of material that community members can search; nothing ever goes out of print.

6. Such a publication has virtually unlimited space for reader comment and interaction.

7. Given the nature of the Internet, the publisher can measure reader interest and advertising response in a depth and detail that's not practical for a paper-and-ink publication.

What's in It for You?

E-communities can be excellent places for companies to advertise and participate in the discussions. A potential advertiser, for example, can check out Babble's audience analysis page. The day I visited, the page said that Babble had 1.2 million monthly visits . . . the audience was 80 percent female, 20 percent male . . . 82 percent of the audience was between 25 and 40 years old...median household income was $94,000 . . . and 43 percent of the audience was planning to have more children. If you market goods or services for babies or new parents, you'd want to at least check out Babble. Or, like Kimberly-Clark, you might have your own branded e-communities and look into other social web opportunities, as well. Hasbro sent 5,000 members of the CafeMom community Kid Motion toy kits, which retail for $53. Hasbro suggested the moms talk up the kit when swapping tips about "how to make play fun and enriching." The moms responded: "We are right now playing with the bee jumper! So much fun!" wrote one of the 11,020 members of the Playskool groups.[4]

It's important to distinguish e-communities from, say, the social networking communities of MySpace or YouTube. E-communities largely contain professional content with a leaven of reader comment, whereas the other communities mix user-generated with some professional content. My view is there will be a continual mix for the next few years, but the line is becoming blurrier all the time.

Still, e-communities are going to be an increasingly important digital-only category for connecting with and maintaining some kind of relationship with your most valued customer groups. Now this is where paid advertising can really pay off on the Web. I see advertising becoming more diffused: not all the money will be going into reaching the vast television audience—instead, marketers will be spending to reach highly targeted audiences, putting much smaller amounts of money into advertising about, say, bass fishing in northern Idaho or bass fishing in Mississippi.

Start thinking this way and all sorts of opportunities open up when you look for e-communities. Suppose a car enthusiast subscribes to *Motor Trend* (or *Car and Driver*). On motortrend.com, he can read blogs about the latest Motown news, car designs, concept cars, and more; subscribe to the magazine's e-newsletter and add his two cents to several discussion forums. From videos of the magazine's road tests to virtual road tests and simulations, this car guy will feel like he's at the wheel on the open road, at the track, or wherever.

Still on motortrend.com, he can see the magazine's video coverage of the latest car shows, car-related entertainment, and new car models; download Motor Trend Radio podcasts; vote in online polls; subscribe to the print or electronic version of the magazine. He can compare and price new and used vehicles with just a couple of clicks (and look for car insurance at the same time). Nearly all of this is professional content that covers the vast spectrum of car enthusiasts' interests. And those are just the links from one of the many car-related sites. Various ads for car-related goods and services share the screen with much of the content I've outlined here (caranddriver.com is another example).

Marketers should be aware of the opportunities that tie communities together or cut across communities. So cars lead naturally to communities about cars (or trucks or SUVs) and racing (NASCAR, Formula One, whatever), cars and in-dash entertainment centers, cars and tricked-out accessories, cars and tires, cars and driving, cars and insurance, cars and luggage carriers, cars and ski racks, cars and bicycle racks, antique cars and trucks, car shows, car clubs, car movies, cars and travel, cars and repair services.

Marketers have to be at the intersections where interest areas connect with other topics. Because if you're not at those intersections in the e-community, someone else is going to be there. If Goodrich Tires wasn't advertising on caranddriver.com, then Michelin should be. Same for auto insurance and all the other intersections that make sense for the car enthusiast e-community.

Throw Your Own Party

For years we've been on this drug of mass media, thinking that the more money we invest in television spots, the more we'll sell. I just don't see it. Madison Avenue will continue to fight for television spots, arguing that the numbers are there. But even though viewership is off the charts for the Super Bowl (not to mention the price of 30-second spots), does that mean ads during the Super Bowl sell that much more beer . . . or cars . . . or sneakers? Here's an alternative.

Instead of spending all your advertising money on a fun beer ad, why not divert some to the Web? Suppose you're Under Armour, maker of activewear and athletic shoes. Because your mission is "to make all athletes better," your e-community might focus on skills training, tips from top coaches, and advice from pro players. In fact, Under Armour has aired commercials during the Super Bowl and it also sponsors special events to bring big-league training to ordinary jocks around the country. As of this writing, however, its site is not set up as an e-community encouraging online interaction. I think that's a missed opportunity.

Start building a community, don't just try to sell. Get away from the idea that you have to use television, radio, and print ads to tell people to just buy, buy, buy. Tell them more about the sports you love, and people will come to your special e-community. Bring in complementary content from the NFL and other major league sports. Now you've got a number of marketers coming to *your* party and bringing their professional content to intrigue your community's members.

I believe that this is where marketing is going. Draw millions of people to an e-community and many marketers will want to come to that party. If it's your party, you can charge for advertising space or take a small commission for every sale made by one of your online partners. If it's not your party, you can arrange to be invited and join the discussion with blogs or forums or other content. The cross connections are there for you to explore.

E-Communities Expand the World

The significance of the e-community for the car enthusiast or the DIYer or the skier or anybody is that it's incredibly easy to make these connections, hear other people's opinions, participate, and share. Before, you might have heard about a car show because you read about it in the local paper or you were on somebody's mailing list. But nondigital communication was a lot less efficient and a lot less appealing in some ways (and certainly a lot more hit or miss).

The time is coming when we will share our interests with people for certain periods. Take my car enthusiast example. He—or she—will be able to say, "For the next hour I am going to entertain offers. You know I'm interested in cars or trucks or vans, you know generally how much I spend and what I like. Make me an offer." Rather than the current situation where airlines and hotel chains are offering last-minute, weekend deals, the consumer consciously decides when he or she is ready to entertain business offers.

If I were a marketer in the pharmaceutical/life sciences industries, I'd want to ensure a presence in the most topical e-communities that draw millions of people, such as WebMD's different communities. How do I get my firm included in the chats and the presentations, articles, white papers, and the podcasts? If I were Pfizer, I'd want the senior medical executive for high cholesterol drugs on a podcast talking about the latest advancements in those drugs. The idea is to develop programs and campaigns for getting your company's name, content, and information into the e-communities where your target audiences regularly go.

In the past, you might have felt your company had to be in a relevant magazine, or on a television news show, or on the newspaper's health page. Now you want to participate in the appropriate e-community. Even if you can't actually get onto the site except through paid advertising, you certainly can be linked in their stories. How about cooperating via your site? For car enthusiasts, BMW can offer blogs, videos, podcasts, interviews, sneak peeks, and much more.

Add Your Voice

Another way to use e-communities is through the chat rooms. Become familiar with the various e-community chat rooms where your customers go, so you can try to interest some of those audiences in coming to your party. If people are regularly logging onto WebMD and spending time there, how can Genzyme attract them to its party? Try sharing information in the chat areas, or the bulletin boards, or posting questions. Or participate in the e-community's blog to raise awareness of your company and what it's doing. If somebody is commenting on the WebMD site or any other site and there's a place for comment, you can comment as well. You can comment on the comments. The thread keeps going, and, on the Web, it exists forever. Make yourself part of the e-community conversation.

Previously, the only way you could interact with a magazine if you were an everyday Joe was send a letter to the editor and hope it got printed. In an e-community, the everyday Joes and the marketing professionals both have far more potential for a far more influential voice in what is going on.

Of course, certain e-communities are quasi-professional. As I said a few pages ago, the line between categories is increasingly blurry. Some e-communities border on a combination of blogs and professional content. In your Observe phase, therefore, you have to identify not only the significant bloggers but also the growing e-communities of professional content that can influence audiences important to your marketing efforts.

Look at their content. What are they trying to do? Most of them will tell you. What can you add? Most editors are hungry for new information, new leads, new voices. All successful companies have experts and thought leaders whose ideas and observations would be of interest to the editors and the writers of the e-communities.

E-communities will become the preferred resource for today's generation the way magazines were for an older generation. The parents of yesterday had *Parents*, the parents of today have Babble.com as well as the print and e-community versions of *Parents*. The older generation had *Forbes*, the new generation has Forbes.com. The big difference is that in the older world, magazines, newspapers, radio, and television were one-way communication. In the e-communities, members take only what they want, take as much as they want, and talk back. One more time: *Marketing is a dialogue.*

The Social Networks Strategy

(Connecting with a Click)

Talk about a level playing field: marketing to social networks is a viable strategy for businesses large and small. You don't need deep pockets to get the conversation going, either. Remember BlendTec's "Will It Blend?" videos, which I talked about in Chapter 8? They're all made on a shoestring, yet the series has attracted more than 60 million viewers. Who can resist clicking to watch a CEO gleefully pulverize an iPhone or a *Grand Theft Auto* disc?

Of course, if you've got a big budget, social networking sites can add even more punch to your marketing effort. Think of the annual hoopla over Super Bowl commercials, for example. Leading up to the game, YouTube and other video sites post sneak previews of some commercials. During and after the game, hundreds of thousands of people jump online to debate about the commercials, share their favorites, see what reviewers say, and add their voices to the discussion. One YouTube video, a loop of the top 10 commercials from last year's Super Bowl, drew nearly a million views. These viewers were clicking to watch seven-and-a-half minutes of nothing but ads!

Clearly, it's a vid, vid, vid, vid world. The last time I checked, the most popular video on YouTube was comedian Judson Laipply's *Evolution of Dance*. It's been viewed more than 90 million times. That's Super Bowl-sized viewership for a video that's only a few minutes long. And the audience for online videos is growing day by day. Already, according to Hitwise, some 10 million people visit online video sites during any given month. YouTube is far and away the most popular video site; MySpaceTV, Google Video, Yahoo Video, and Veoh round out the top five.[1]

"Marketers are trying to increase the quality of the experiences visitors have on their marketing sites, and video is becoming a really important part of that," says my friend Jeremy Allaire, the CEO of Brightcove, a software service company. "Video is a great way to express a brand. They can provide deep exploration of the product and can have a lot of educational content. Video is format that consumers understand and like, so many marketers are investing in more and more video as a way to increase the odds that a consumer takes an interest in their product."

Jeremy points out that ranges across diverse industries, consumer, business-to-business, and both. The Kohler site, for example, has videos on kitchens and baths and on portable power generation systems. The Kohler TV network has hundreds of short programs, says Jeremy, everything from ideas on how to use their products to sophisticated understanding of the technology to aesthetic pieces about what your life can be like with their products. "The content focuses on the dealer side, because most kitchen and bath products are brought to consumers by people who install them. The site has grown and grown in terms of usage and is becoming a central piece of Kohler's marketing and sales efforts."

Reid Hoffman, the founder of the LinkedIn social network, observes that bringing video contact online is similar to the print-to-television revolution. "Suddenly this is a much more emotionally and socially engaging medium. There is much more social interaction for me to be watching someone's own little music video than to be reading a long blog post."

One difficulty some marketers have with video on the social web is that they tend to think of commercials. Online video can be infinitely richer than a one-minute sales pitch. "One of the most common questions we hear," says Jeremy, "is what content could we create that would be so engaging people would want to spread it around? It would be a way to get awareness at a much lower cost than buying TV advertising. It becomes a barrier to adoption, because sometimes marketers think they need to do something incredibly creative if they are going to use video." In fact, an online video can be informative (how we manufacturer our product), educational (how to install our product in your home), entertaining (make the Subservient Chicken dance), or all three.

BlendTec may not have the marketing budget of Super Bowl advertisers like Pepsi or Budweiser, but its homemade videos sure are engaging. More to the point, they've boosted brand recognition and sent sales soaring. But you don't have to have video content to build or reinforce brand recognition, connect with your targeted audiences, and leverage your marketing messages using a social networks strategy.

Everything Old Is New Again

By now you know that social networks are member-based online communities that enable users to link to one another based on common interests. They have mainly user-generated content, although they may also have material produced by professionals or experts. In addition to YouTube, well-known examples include MySpace, Facebook, Flikr, and more. Popular social networks outside the United States include Orkut, Mixi, Hyves, and Friendster (which is particularly strong in Asia).

Nonvirtual social networks have been around for centuries. From the Industrial Revolution until fairly recently, much of life outside of work involved people in social networks like the church, the lodge, the Lions, Elk, Moose, Odd Fellows, Masons, bowling leagues, sewing circles, bridge clubs, political clubs, and much, much more. Networks with a professional angle—such as Rotary, Kiwanis, and thousands of industry-specific organizations—are all "social networks" in their nature. Also, what's been the most popular place on a college campus throughout the past hundred years? (Hint: Not the library.) Probably the student union, although fraternities and sororities are also forms of social networks.

While such social networks never went away, they certainly declined after World War II. As Harvard sociologist Robert Putnam wrote in his seminal 1995 book *Bowling Alone*: "Television, two-career families, suburban sprawl, generational changes in values—these and other changes in American society have meant that fewer and fewer of us find that the League of Women Voters, or the United Way, or the Shriners, or the monthly bridge club, or even a Sunday picnic with friends fits the way we have come to live."[2]

The extraordinary growth of social networks on the Web suggests that many people recognize a human need for such connections and are trying to find them as best they can. The technology industry, especially the software industry, which is only about 30 years old, started "user groups" early on. A company like Lotus or Microsoft or Oracle would pay to bring its software users together to enjoy speakers and educational content, refreshments, and entertainment as a way to spread the word about the software. After a few years, company sponsorship dropped off as users started paying their own way because they wanted to spend time with other users, giving and getting the latest tips and tricks.

Even as we had become desocialized for all the reasons Putman identified, when we were spending more time alone and developing a more focused interests in specific topics like games, sex, medicine, sports, and more, there was a breakthrough in the digital realm. Given the human drive for community, it makes sense that we would evolve and create some kind of digital social atmosphere.

Click and Connect

The first online social networks really began in 1999 with a company called Emode, founded by James Currier. Emode (which changed its name to Tickle) was a pioneer in getting people to fill out questionnaires online. What is your interest? What do you like to do? The software would then match people within a community based on similar interests. That was a surprisingly brave new idea way back when. Tickle was eventually bought by Monster.com and today, as part of Monster's Affinity Labs, offers millions of members more than 200 personality, career, and entertainment tests, promising to deliver "a deep, rich, and meaningful way for people to connect with one another."

For marketers, Tickle offers a convenient way to reach out to a self-selected group of prospective customers and understand their demographic, personality, career, and behavioral characteristics. Not long ago, Procter & Gamble's Cover Girl brand turned to Tickle to reach teen girls and young women, extend its seasonal "color" promotions online, and build a database. Tickle developed a series of seasonal themed beauty quizzes relevant to Cover Girl's products and embedded an opt-in question in the quizzes to build the database. The results (at least the ones that P&G will reveal): 5 percent of the young women who took the quizzes clicked through to Cover Girl, and opt-ins averaged over 2,000 a week during the promotion.

In many ways, Amazon was an early social network. Although it had a specific commercial goal—to sell lots of books—the architecture was one of community. The idea was that you got to know the site, the people, the things that were happening, what people were saying, what was available to buy, and join the conversation. Amazon wasn't (isn't) just an online retailer selling you books, it was soliciting your opinion about the books (and, now, everything else it sells).

Then Friendster went live in 2003, and because it was ready-made for uploaded images, the burgeoning digital camera craze made Friendster more successful than the older Six Degrees (which managed to attract about 10 million people but could not get them to come back). Social networks are increasingly popular for personal and professional use. Now, says Reid Hoffman of LinkedIn, "you have the ability to browse your social network and find out interesting things about who people really are. Some of that is about dating, about 'Is the person cute?' But also some of it is about making the whole thing much more human."

The wired world is taking full advantage of well, how our brains are wired to recognize and respond to faces and interpersonal interaction. Now people can take and swap both still and moving images from their digital cameras, video cameras, cell phones, and laptops. As the technology improves, the pictures will improve and the whole social network experience will become that much richer. Already, for many people, participation in one or more social networks is taking the place of watching television or reading a book or a magazine.

I don't think peoples' nature has changed that much; despite our busy, modern lifestyles, we are still social beings. The venue today is more digital than the Grange Hall or the church basement. If you buy my argument that human beings really want to belong to specific types of social networks, and if you also buy my argument that the Web is increasingly the next-closest thing to physical life without actually being in another person's presence, you understand the phenomenal growth of online social networks.

Think Interests, Not Just Demographics

This changing face of social networks really means that people like to belong to certain communities. They like the information and they like the people even though they are not physically meeting them. Not everyone, of course. I've heard people of a certain age say, "Talking to a stranger online sounds really scary." Well, yes, it can be. But how many times have you waited for a bus or been in an elevator or stood in a supermarket line and carried on a five-minute conversation with a stranger? Maybe something connected, or maybe you had nothing in common and that was the end of the connection.

But technology has the ability to capture patterns in people's behaviors and connect you to other people with similar interests and backgrounds. Think of Amazon's ability, based on your buying behavior, to suggest books in which you might be interested or Netflix's ability to suggest movie titles. Or Tickle's ability to connect you to others based on your answers to a quiz.

Social network sites include wine clubs, sports clubs, recipe exchanges, so it's not just MySpace, Facebook, and YouTube. If I were head of marketing at Gallo or Beringer or Kendall Jackson, I would want to be in front of people in the wine clubs, alerting them to this week's tasting sessions in, say, Albany, Indianapolis, and Oklahoma City. I would like to let them know there are discounts on my cases in these 37 states. But don't ever forget that the community controls the club itself. The community decides whether there will be commercial messages, based on the site's need for revenue and service to the members.

Also remember that social networks are all about common interests. The social networking site Eons found this out the hard way. Originally designed for the 50-plus demographic, Eons drew a lot of traffic through well-placed paid search ads. However, according to the *New York Times,* visitors who clicked through these ads stared at the Eons site for only a few seconds before clicking away. On the other hand, members who came for the information, such as best places to retire and favorite travel destinations, lingered for an average of 20 minutes per visit.

Jeff Taylor, the founder of Eons, recently tweaked the site by eliminating the age limitation and focusing instead on members' interests. By this time, members had already taken the initiative to form 3,000 groups around shared interests like taking cruises and moving to Florida. "The fate of Eons will hinge on whether boomers want to patronize online destinations that treat them as a distinct g-g-generation," concluded the *Times's* Randall Stross.[3] So look beyond demographics to focus on interests.

Focus on Focused Social Networks

The next generation of consumer social networks has much smaller, far more focused networks—which helps the midsize and small marketer as well as the biggest enterprises. Pick some sort of very specific interest related to your product or service, be it model trains, home brewing, or scrapbooking; find the social networks in that arena; and see how you can participate.

Focused social networks are what Ning (ning.com) is all about. Ning provides the technology for anyone to get a social network going about anything. Already it's the online home of more than 250,000 social networks, and co-founder Marc Andreessen (of Netscape fame) says it's growing at the rate of 1,000 new networks per day.[4]

One Ning-based network, "Meet the Phlockers," connects 5,000 fans of Jimmy Buffet and others who share a tropical frame of mind. The day I visited, I saw ads featuring concert tickets and Key West vacations—very targeted offers for Parrot Heads in particular.

Another Ning-based network, "Firefighter Nation," is an online gathering place for 21,000 firefighters, EMS, and rescue personnel. Within Firefighter Nation are a wide variety of special interest groups, such as Fitness for Emergency Services and Junior Firefighters of Kentucky, which each attract anywhere from a handful of members to several hundred members. Among the ads I saw on this social network's home page was one for firefighter ringtones, one for firefighter artwork, and one for used firefighting equipment.

You can see where Ning is going and why advertisers might want to go there, too. In the words of *Fast Company* magazine: "Ning wants to foster millions of little networks with narrow channels, each delivering the kind of targeted advertising that Google rode to vast riches." In short, it's not about how many eyeballs, but "the kind of eyeballs you collect and how you can slice, dice, and model them."[5]

The focused social network strategy is not just for consumer goods marketing; it's also profoundly useful for business-to-business marketing. Dentists, doctors, butchers, bakers, and candlestick makers all may have an interest in social networks. LinkedIn is one of the best-known business-to-business social networks. However, if you're a large enterprise, you can start creating an online destination around what you do, your products, and your technology, tapping into the interests of your customer base. (Pick up a highlighter and look back at the chapters in Part II for a start.)

As a business-to-consumer example, think about the narrow focus of Genzyme, which works to discover successful drug therapies for rare diseases. If my child had a rare disease, I would want to know about the Genzyme community. I'd want to know why it costs so much to develop a drug for my child's disease. I'd want to meet other parents with children suffering from the same illness. For Genzyme to facilitate those contacts and bring me that information would be much more powerful for Genzyme than if I were to obtain it somewhere else, say from Google or from raredisease.org.

The opportunity here is to show that you're an important community source for authentic information, not just marketing hype. In the business-to-business world, IBM has been in a business machine and computing technology company longer than anybody on the planet and has more patents in its fields than anybody else. So if you're a technology/software buyer, you would reason that IBM must have something thoughtful to say to you or help you. Maybe you're thinking of buying new servers and you wonder whether you should use open source software . . . IBM has the credibility to offer answers and host this kind of valuable content.

A Slow Build, Not a Quick Transaction

It's tempting to go for the quick transaction: One click on Amazon and you've bought the book. However, what MySpace, Facebook, and YouTube have taught us about the social network is that you don't have to go for the transaction right away. Create an attractive environment and community; invite people to come, spend some time, meet some people, share some stories, download some content, and you know what . . . you'll probably sell stuff.

It's not just about advertising, it's about links to other things, talking about products, talking about experiences: Did you see the latest Will It Blend video? Did you take that Cover Girl beauty quiz? If people feel comfortable in a social network setting, and even if it is on a company site, they trust you. They are going to share information.

The other lesson from YouTube, MySpace, and Facebook is that our ideas of privacy are in flux. Some people complain about a lack of privacy, but others are videoing themselves in their bedrooms talking about their so-called lives, disclosing everything about their friends or makeup or body-building. Don't judge it. It's the behavior of the next generation—your customers are doing it, watching it, blogging about it. The real issue is: How do you act in a more social way, rather than a transactional way, to create a brand?

You have to start with some kind of architecture, and I would argue that you have to think about a social network the way you think about a building. The better architect you are, the better social network you will have. Don't confuse this with the software itself. Many companies use proprietary technology but you can also go to companies like, Ning, Neighborhood America (neighborhoodamerica.com), and Kick Apps (kickapps.com) for social networking software.

For example, HGTV hired Neighborhood America to build "Rate My Space," a social networking site where people post photos of their home improvement projects for visitors to rate and discuss. The site, at ratemyspace.hgtv.com, is a unique branded place where HGTV can engage people, entertain people, and help people. The site became so popular that it spawned a "Rate My Space" HGTV cable show, sponsored by Lowe's. And remember, HGTV didn't have to know anything about the technical side of putting up a networking site.

A word about creating special spaces for people. When I appeared in a PBS special about the future of the library, I said libraries have a big future. Almost everybody else on the show disagreed: Who needs a library when you have Google and the Internet? The historian David McCullough and I believe the library has a big future. One of the main reasons I emphasized was the need to be in a special place. When I was a child, there were two very special places I would go— to church and the library. The library was quiet, orderly, a place of thoughtful contemplation full of people who enjoyed the same experience. The architect had to provide different places for people with different interests: the children's corner, the history area, biography section, fiction shelves, poetry, and so on.

Behavior has not changed that much. The power of creating spaces that people want to come to, want to feel good in, is all part of this movement of social networks and the building of communities. Companies have a right—even a responsibility—to build their own communities and provide spaces for their customers to talk to one another, places for them to learn (using tools like podcasts and microsites). Of course, these communities are places where visitors control what they see, say, do, contribute.

So if you're Pfizer, you want to create a space for a community of physicians, patients, caregivers, insurance companies, and legislators. If you're Whirlpool, you want a community of dealers, distributors, service technicians, suppliers, and regulators. If you're JPMorgan Chase, you want a community of investors, regulators, customers, media contacts, and financial advisors.

The earlier you embark on the architecture of your own enterprise social network, the better it will become over time as your community tells you what they like, what they don't like, what you see working, what you measure, where you go. I know this is a big revolution. I argue the Internet itself will prove to have more impact than television, radio, or any media that have come before. Social networks will prove to be the most powerful tool for both the social side and the working/business side of online marketing.

What I find fascinating is that social networks are so young and growing so rapidly. Think how many years the Internet took to become as sophisticated as newspapers, magazines, radio, and television have become and now how fast the digital world is evolving. What are later generations of social networks going to look like? I believe they'll be geared to very narrow interests, more like Ning's networks than MySpace and Facebook giants. Many will be enterprise sites with special places to share information with others and watch or download useful or entertaining material—places where visitors are part of the dialogue, not simply passive observers.

Another promising development is the way technology enables people to cut across social networking boundaries. Until recently, your MySpace page had to be separate from your Facebook page, your Flickr photos, your YouTube videos, or your Twitter tweets. Now MySpace allows you to show content from your MySpace on eBay, for instance, or on another site. Facebook has a similar feature. And third-party tech specialists like Flock and Chirp Interactive have software to let you browse and follow what friends are doing on Twitter, Facebook, MySpace, and other sites with a glance. Will this be super-convenient or will it cause super-overload? It's too soon to tell.

Organizing for the Social Web

How do you adapt the traditional marketing department organization to embrace the opportunities inherent in social networks? Even if CEOs enthusiastically embrace the ideas in this book, they have to obtain the marketing department's cooperation, and that may require a major shuffling of responsibilities. I have noticed some firms organizing to build a community as an integral part of their marketing. This shows up in titles such as "Chief Community Builder" or "Vice President of Communities."

If I were organizing the marketing department to take advantage of the social web, I would first want to be clear about the customer map (which I talked about in Chapter 5) and understand the environment in which my company operates. I would formulate the marketing plan with a long-term campaign perspective in mind. What do we want to accomplish over time in building the communities we envision and what kind of content are we going to need today and tomorrow?

At the top of the marketing pyramid, chief marketing officers (CMOs) will become more like television or movie producers. Instead of having directors of public relations and of advertising, they'll need a director, cinematographer, sound person, set designer, costume designer, makeup artist, editor, key grip, and best boy. CMOs, who remain responsible for product development and new markets, will have two czars as direct reports: the director of unpaid (social) media and the director of paid media. Ideally, these three managers would work together in planning everything the marketing department will do.

The responsibilities for the director of unpaid media would be community-building, content, customer mapping, analytics and behavior, competitive analysis, competitive landscaping, new media, digital and traditional media relations, and customer care (specifically, customer care content). Also, this executive would be responsible for the organization's search engine optimization, corporate blogs, e-community (or communities), and social networks.

The director of paid media would be responsible for advertising, trade shows, events, loyalty programs, experiential marketing, product placement, and all the promotional materials that the organization has always done. In terms of social networks, the paid media person would be responsible for bringing people to the community, paid opportunities to advertise on television or print or on the Web, direct marketing, and so on. Digital direct marketing and e-mail marketing would be a part of paid media. Search, online banners, buttons, and ads are part of paid media.

I would add third-party relations (analyst communities, partners, etc.) to the marketing department's duties. I'd have somebody in charge of organic and paid search, including responsibility for monitoring all the search engines to make sure the company is properly represented. If the company had plenty of resources, I might have somebody who monitored customer conversations. (If we're allowing customers to post on our site, we do need to screen out obscene, libelous, and inappropriate comments.) What was public relations would now be digital media and community building or new media relations.

Clearly such changes would be a wrench, because advertising in the past was measured by cost per thousand (CPM). While new measurements will include CPM, marketers will now be checking metrics measuring engagement and downloads, for example. How long did a given visitor stay on our site? Who did she interact with? What did she do? Did she download a podcast? Did she watch or download a video? What page did she first view on our site and where did she go when she left the site?

For simplicity, I'd categorize marketing functions in terms of observe, engage, and measure. *Observe* covers all the behavioral and analytics and data about customers, prospects, and competitors. *Engage* covers all the campaigns, the creative, and the community content. *Measure* covers the engagement metrics and the downloads. Some important metrics, as I suggested in the last paragraph, are the number of customers coming to the community and their regular interactions within the community. You'll be able to measure these just as traditional bricks-and-mortar retailers are able to ask people as they walk out of the store, "Did you find what you came for? Were the sales associates helpful? Are you satisfied? Would you recommend our store to your friends and family?"

Similarly, after a customer has been in the digital environment, you could ask: "Did you like it? What would you change? How would you make this better, richer, more rewarding? Would you e-mail a friend about your experience on the site? What did you like most? What did like least? Is there anything you absolutely hated? What content would you like to see that wasn't there?"

All these questions—and the organization's genuine response to them—can make a richer community, with more experiences, more downloadable content, more sharing of content, and more dialogue with and among customers.

Does Facebook Matter?

(To Marketers?)

Facebook has tapped into a real interest and desire to connect, something to which teens and twenty-something young adults in particular readily respond. Founded at Harvard in 2004 exclusively for college students (a requirement it dropped in late 2006), Facebook had almost eight million members just three years later, fueled solely by word of mouse.

Facebook is such a fast-moving phenomenon that it's hard to say exactly how big it is. David Wilkins, senior director of content strategy at the social networking solutions firm Mzinga, writes that in "an analysis of the most recent Facebook advertising data, over 50 percent of the 20- to 30-year-olds in the U.S. have Facebook accounts (based on a comparison of Facebook's ad data and U.S. Census Bureau numbers.)"[1] Yes, *more than half* of all Americans in the 20–30 age group.

Of course, not everyone who has a Facebook account will be an active user. One source (www.allfacebook.com) said in June 2008 that

the site had more than 70 million total users. Another (www.trendrr
.com) found the number of *daily* users in late June ranging from
around 250,000 to 315,000 (perhaps because school was out?).

While both sources may be correct and looking at different parts
of the elephant, a blogger named Paul Francis went to the trouble of
gathering Facebook user data via an advertiser tool that facilitates
audience targeting. In November 2007, he pulled user numbers for
the top countries, broken down by male/female. He found a total of
42,966,780 Facebook members in the top 31 countries. The U.S. had
the most users, just over 18 million, 60 percent of whom were female.[2]
comScore, a research company that measures Internet traffic among
other things, reported that Facebook had 123.9 million unique worldwide visitors in May 2008, and 50.6 billion page views. By comparison, MySpace had 114.5 million visitors and 45.4 billion page views.[3]

Interestingly, comScore attempted to track the ages of Facebook visitors a while ago and if the figures have remained at all consistent, the
site is not attracting young people only. comScore reported that about
15 percent of the unique visitors to the site in May 2007 were ages 15 to
17; about 30 percent were ages 18 to 24; 12 percent were 25 to 34; and
almost 40 percent were over 35. (The numbers do not add to 100.)[4]

Apart from the numbers, which are huge, the first point I want
to make is that Facebook is not so much a social network as it is a
new communications platform. That's especially true for a generation
that wants to stay in touch with a group of friends or acquaintances
without having to individually update every person. A Facebook
profile is something like an e-mail with a cc list. Compared with the
software platform tools I discussed in the last chapter—such as Ning,
Neighborhood America, or KickApps—Facebook is an even more
convenient operating environment for posting and sharing thoughts,
ideas, pictures, videos, and original songs.

The other thing about Facebook is that most of its millions
and millions of members communicate with relatively few people.
My daughter comes home and posts to the same kid she just talked
to at school. But she adds her fifteen-year-old cousin who lives in
another state and some other friends that she doesn't see all the time.
Although I call Facebook this generation's mass media, it is highly

segmentable into smaller audiences and I think it will naturally evolve into micro-segmented content as well.

Just as we got used to e-mail quickly, I see a generation getting used to Facebooking. They can e-mail if they have to, but they would rather post six, seven, eight times a day. It almost becomes a student union of the mind while they're constantly going between classes. I believe Facebook will become even more popular than it is today, with different flavors for different communities. It's still learning how to monetize itself. At the same time, Facebook is defining an age of non-intrusive marketing—and exactly how marketers are going to do that effectively, create demand without banging prospects over the head with sales messages—is still up in the air.

Getting Started on Facebook

How can your company get started on Facebook? Ethan Beard, Facebook's director of business development, says the first step in using Facebook as an effective marketing tool is free and easy: Create a business presence using Facebook Pages, a presence over which you have complete control. "You can build your presence and interact with users, communicate with users, and allow users to become fans and connect with that brand," he explains. (A fan, in Facebook-speak, is a member who joins a Facebook Page.) The site already hosts more than 150,000 Facebook Pages featuring businesses large and small, local and international.

Next, check out the paid services that Facebook offers to tap into targeting and demographic information and find your brand's fans. "If your business is looking for females, aged 34 to 43, who live in San Francisco and are interested in cooking, you can deliver your message just to these people," says Ethan. Now you can harness word-of-mouse to reach friends of those fans. "For example, if I become a fan of Apple," says Ethan, "Apple can take that message and accelerate that through my friends and attach a commercial message to it."

What you do next depends on your marketing goals, your brand or product, and your fans. There's a world of possibilities, as examples later in this chapter demonstrate, once you've established your presence.

A word of advice: Whatever you do as a marketer on Facebook, do it carefully. As Greg Andersen, director of engagement planning for North America at BBH (Bartle Bogle Hegarty), writes: "Brands run the risk of looking like I must have looked to my niece when I joined Facebook and sent her a friend invite: An outsider trying to seem with it, unsure of why we're there or what we're supposed to do to become a valuable member of the community. We're the awkward adults with disposable income but no idea what's really going on around us. But we're there, damn it. And that makes us cool. We bought the sneakers and the ironic T-shirt. We're one of you. Want to be friends?

"Not only do they not want to be friends, they increasingly don't even want to be in the same room as us. Pizza Hut has a page on Facebook. Why? I mean, who wants to be friends with a pizza?"

Andersen argues that young people are moving from one place to another at mind-numbing speeds. And bad marketing is "part of the reason that people like my niece are leaving one setting and moving on to the next new thing where we're not clumsily asking them if they want to be friends. The social-networking environment is littered with irrelevant brand applications." Andersen says that brands and their agencies have often jumped into trendy environments to do trendy things without asking: What are we doing here? Why is it right for the brand? How does it align to a meaningful objective? Is it really something the people we're talking to will do? How does it add value for them?[5]

David Berkowitz, the director of emerging media and client strategy at 360i, a digital marketing agency, makes the often-overlooked point that Facebook's users visit the site first and foremost to communicate with each other. They're not there to buy anything. Facebook is not a search engine that people use to look for information about a product or brand. Facebook is not like reading the *New York Times* online or watching MSNBC, where people expect the experience to be supported by advertising. Even though the business model of Facebook might work the same way, it's still a new medium and is entirely social. David cautions that members resent anything that smacks of commercialism—especially if it's untargeted.

On Facebook: Victoria's Secret and the *New York Times*

Victoria's Secret Pink was one of the first brands to get hundreds of thousands of people involved in its Facebook Page (it recently had almost 400,000 fans). Pink is a line of casual wear (sweat pants, tee shirts, jackets, hoodies) targeted to college students; college logos are available on everything. David Berkowitz explains: "The page had fans submit photos; it held contests; and it offered electronic wallpaper, icons, fun things like that. The page served as a way for people who were fans or should have been fans to connect and to express themselves."

Pink's Facebook page is very PG, not sexy in any way. Recently the site had three short kid-friendly videos. Yet it was one of the early breakthroughs on Facebook because, Dave points out, the brand really resonates with this particular audience: "It's a brand that teenage and college-age girls are going to tell their friends about." They've seen the Victoria's Secret store at the mall, they've tried on Pink apparel, and the Facebook presence gives them a chance to play with the brand's playful side.

Another example: The *New York Times* is attracting an older audience on Facebook. Its page features a news trivia quiz, five multiple-choice questions on the day's news that let you compete with your friends for the best score (and there were 2,500 daily active users at its peak). The fun fits the brand and encourages interaction with the *Times* page as well as with friends, which is why this is a good use of Facebook's functionality.

Let's Talk Turkey and Tea

Here are a few more examples of how companies are engaging Facebook members. Last June, the National Turkey Federation gave fans a chance to "talk turkey" during its Turkey Lovers' Month. The federation says it chose Facebook "to reach a younger audience that is talking with their peers through this social networking community."

Members were invited to add a turkey "voki"—a small, talking avatar turkey—to their personal Facebook pages and share it with their friends. (You can create your own speaking avatar at—where else?—voki.com.)

This voki campaign combined a number of social-networking features to accelerate word-of-mouse. First, it didn't take itself too seriously. The voki wore a T-shirt saying "Shake Your Tail Feather" and had a repertoire of sayings like: "Do I make you hungry? Happy Turkey Month!"

Second, it was customizable and interactive. Users could personalize the talking turkey's clothes and could even upload their own voice to make the voki speak. And third, the turkey was tagged with the federation's eatturkey.com URL, in case curious Facebook members wanted to know more.

Another good example of marketing through Facebook comes from R.C. Bigelow, the specialty tea company. Bigelow has been involved in blogging and social networking for a couple of years. Its Facebook Page includes videos starring CEO Cindi Bigelow, who demonstrates how to naturally decaffeinate tea, how to make a perfect cup of tea, and many other tea tips. She recently told the *New York Times*, "I'm young, 47, and it's fun for me to do videos so that people can put a face and personality to Bigelow Tea."

Getting personal is the point of Bigelow's Facebook marketing. "There are not a lot of family-owned companies that are national. It's great that we have this opportunity to let the consumer get to know us, and it's another way we can get to know them," the CEO explains. "I've always called consumers personally if they had a problem. So using the new media is an extension of a philosophy we already knew—take care of your customers, talk to them. I create videos and young people respond with their own. I watch a few every week and laugh. It's so great to see a 23-year-old from the middle of the country holding up her box of Bigelow Tea. How great is it to be able to see all kinds of people, with their own styles, wanting to talk about Bigelow Tea on the Internet?"[6]

Here's another example, this time from the beer industry. Coors Brewing invited consumers of drinking age to send their friends

"Code Blue" alerts on Facebook. "Code Blue" refers to the bottle's label, which changes color when the beer is cold enough to drink. Members might send a "Code Blue" inviting friends to meet for a Coors Light at a nearby bar, for instance, and attach a Facebook map so nobody gets lost.

Facebook was only one part of the overall campaign, which included television commercials and a MySpace presence. Coors calls this "360-ing"—using all forms of media to reach potential customers—and whether or not they were a big hit, the Facebook alerts were part of the learning process. When it comes to the new media, Coors CMO Andy England says, "Everyone, particularly in offline businesses like ours, is still in a very experimental phase. We, along with our agencies, are trying to learn what works best and expand on those ideas."

Creating a special application for Facebook makes sense because the site "is so adept at bringing people together and getting in touch with people quickly throughout the day," according to Tim Sproul, group creative director in the Portland, Ore., office of Avenue A/Razorfish, one of Coors's agencies. "And if you have anything to pitch in a social environment, it makes sense to pitch beer. We feel like we're not intrusive in the online experience; we're relevant, by giving people a chance to connect."[7]

Major banks like JPMorgan Chase have made forays onto Facebook with limited success. "On the surface," writes Christina Rexrode in *The Charlotte Observer*, "tapping into Facebook's reach seems like a potent marketing strategy, a way to meet young people—and lots of them—on their own turf." She found more than 100 credit unions with profile pages, "though most are rudimentary. Intrepid employees at the Service One Credit Union in Bowling Green, Ky., posted photos of an office sock puppet and information about a credit card seminar for students at nearby Western Kentucky University."

The results aren't always pretty. Harsh feedback is virtually guaranteed, says Rexrode: "One four-member Facebook group, apparently started by a student angry over some overdraft fees, says it 'is dedicated to driving the evil JPMorgan Chase Bank into the ground.' The banks, for their part, say they appreciate how Facebook lets customers communicate with them so easily. 'Facebook is a huge brand and innovative medium in which many consumers, particularly a younger demographic, engage with, so it's been an excellent vehicle in which we can have outreach to that particular audience,' said Tanya Madison, a JPMorgan Chase spokeswoman."

Still, Rexrode pointed out, young people seem hesitant to mix Facebook with business. She quoted Matt Nethery, a 24-year-old Charlotte resident who thought the idea of banks on Facebook sounded "cheesy." People log on to get away from work, he said, not to be reminded of their bank accounts. And when the *Online Banking Report*, a trade publication, asked 500 Facebook users whether they'd be interested in viewing their bank account balance through Facebook, 70 percent said "No way."[8]

Doing Business on Facebook

If banks and credit unions are struggling to find a way to engage young Facebook members, Ernst & Young appears to have found the formula. Its Ernst & Young Careers Facebook Page recently had 15,683 fans. On the site, the company says, "Facebook allows us to share the EY experience with people who are interested in the firm, and creates a way for interns and employees to stay in touch with one another. The group provides a forum for people to share their questions, experiences, and comments regarding the Firm, and we can let you know when we're coming to your campus for 'Meet the Firms' nights, career fairs, on-campus interviews and other events."

The page says that E&Y is a professional organization with a social atmosphere, and Facebook provides it with an opportunity to show its fun environment with pictures, comments, and discussions "Don't be shy about adding a comment to the wall [Facebook's name for the place for comments], joining a discussion, or adding pictures to our photo album." A quick review of the comments finds the majority to be serious requests for information (for example, "How do I apply for an internship?" "When are you coming to my campus?") interspersed with a few criticisms (such as "Ernst & Young overworks you and pays very little . . . Go for PWC as your #1 choice.")

What is not allowed in the Facebook group? E&Y's guidelines say: "Discretion is a good rule of thumb. If it's something you wouldn't say at work, or a picture you wouldn't show at work, then it's probably not a good idea to put it on the group page. Comments and photos that are inappropriate for the workplace will be taken down." And because E&Y employees also use the site, "the usual EY privacy rules apply—no mention of specific clients, prospects, or personal details about co-workers. Just as we respect your privacy, we ask that you respect theirs."

Visa is also using Facebook for marketing, this time on the business-to-business side. Its Visa Business Network on Facebook helps small businesses connect with each other and with their customers. To encourage members to join and use the site, Visa planned to award a total of $2 million in Facebook advertising credit ($100 each to 20,000 members) for small business owners to promote their own businesses.

According to the company's statement, this Facebook-based site "can help small business owners easily tap into a global network of peers and advisers from among the more than 80,000 small businesses already on Facebook. It will also provide small business owners with valuable business tools and help them efficiently identify and target thousands of prospective customers. This one-stop resource will empower small business owners to expand their customer base, manage their business better, and exchange ideas with other businesses and trusted advisers."

This Visa-branded Facebook program offers three big benefits to small businesses:

- *Connect with others.* "Networking is an essential part of a small business' success; it helps owners grow and manage their business," says Visa. "The Visa Business Network is a simple way to find and network with other business owners for new business, best practices, advice or support."

- *Manage more efficiently.* "Small business owners can access tool kits from content partners that provide easy-to-use products, including Google Docs, Google Calendar, and Google Sites, to help increase business efficiency. Small business owners can also quickly get an online presence through Google Maps." Via partnerships with *The Wall Street Journal* and *Entrepreneur* magazine, small business owners can "Ask the Experts" and connect with small business authorities by participating in Q&A forums. Visa is providing access to small-business news feeds, videos, blogs, and editorial commentary about issues such as cash flow management, new ways to attract customers, and cost management.

- *Grow the business.* "Small business owners can grow their business by reaching more than 80 million active users worldwide and more than 80,000 small businesses on Facebook," says Visa. "Facebook users communicate and share information through the social graph—digital mapping of the connections and relationships between people that exist in the real world."

Don't Stifle the Dialogue

Marketers want to know how they can control what's said on Facebook and all over the social web. The answer, as I suggested several chapters ago, is: You have very little control. Ernst & Young may have specific guidelines for posting on its Facebook Page, but it can't control what people say about the firm on other Facebook pages or elsewhere online.

This lack of control may not be all bad. David Berkowitz at 360i cites a recent Pepsi promotion on Facebook as an example, a contest in which fans were invited to design their own soda can. Pepsi ran television commercials and put up a microsite as well, "but the beauty of it was the message boards on which people could comment," Dave notes. "Some of the stuff was constructive feedback Pepsi would never have gotten anywhere else. The dark side was that one of the message board posts was called 'facts' and it had people talking about some really dirty stuff. It wasn't the most prominent part of the discussions, but it wasn't hard to find. I give Pepsi a lot of credit for not doing anything to repress that."

Instead of focusing on control, focus on building trust. Facebook's Ethan Beard tells me: "The most important thing marketers need to think about when approaching Facebook is that it is all about building a trust and authentic relationships with the customers who are on Facebook. You need to treat them with respect and you need to engage with them. You can't simply rerun the same ads that you run on any other site, just drop them onto Facebook and expect that to build a trusting and authentic relationship."

Forging relationships with customers takes time. "You can't just pop into Facebook one time, run one campaign, and expect users to feel as if you are engaging with them," Ethan continues. "You need to keep your presence actively engaged so that you can have an ongoing and open conversation with them."

It's possible—almost inevitable—that your Facebook fans will post negative comments or off-tangent information, but it's important that you don't try to stifle it. "When you have actively engaged an audience, your biggest supporters will actually become very vocal and will step up to your defense," Ethan says. "And that is a much stronger message than the message of a brand trying to squelch bad news and keep pushing its own message forward."

And what does all this mean for marketing in the future? What will it be like to live and work in Web 4.0? I have some ideas about that in the next chapter.

Living and Working in Web 4.0

(It's Right Around the Corner)

A s I said in Chapter 1, Web 4.0 is right around the corner. The first phase, Web 1.0, ran from about 1989 to 1995, which was the time of web site building using HTML.

The second phase, Web 2.0, started with the advent of the browser. Netscape, Internet Explorer, and other browsers enabled people to maneuver around the Web, search more effectively, and do e-commerce more efficiently. We saw the rise of Yahoo! and Google. Dot-com companies were hot, hot, hot.

As Web 2.0 started to mature, and before the dot-com bubble burst, companies had planted the seeds for the social web. Think Amazon, think eBay—both of which promoted a social structure in various ways. Amazon invited users to post product reviews and respond to reviews; eBay had buyers rating sellers. It was (and is) a real community thing.

In the past few years, the social web of Web 3.0 has taken hold. As I write, we're not only deeply into it, we're moving to a second generation, a social web tailored more specifically to your interests. Whether you like the Red Sox, want to research diabetes, or collect Star Wars memorabilia, you can connect with your interest on the social web. Companies are just beginning to scatter those seeds now for the next and what I think is the most compelling release of the Web, Web 4.0, the emotive web.

Welcome to the Emotive Web

Web 4.0 is emotive because broadband technology means visual and interactive rich media and because the Web is available everywhere—on your laptop, through your cell phone, or via any gadget that uses Wi-Fi, EV-DO, WiMax, and other access technologies. In terms of the individual's control of and demand for words, images, sound, and interactivity the emotive web is far beyond television or anything that has ever existed.

In particular, what makes Web 4.0 emotive are the personal and business sensations, the idea that the experiences offer not only emotions—joy, curiosity, disgust, happiness—but also a sense of satisfaction and fulfillment.

Now for the 64 gazillion-dollar question: What does Web 4.0 mean to marketers?

It means, if nothing else, that we're currently in a period of transition. "Marketers of all sorts are now being urged to give up the steering wheel to a new breed of consumers who want more control over the ways products are peddled to them," reported Stuart Elliott a couple of years ago while attending a meeting of the Association of National Advertisers. The group, he wrote in the *New York Times*, heard "one speaker after another describe a need to replace decades worth of top-down marketing tactics with bottom-up grass roots approaches."[1] And the social web is where the consumer has the power.

My friend Dan Bruns, executive vice president for services at Mzinga, believes that social media touches everything. It will not be long before every major company has a social web initiative with its customers or its employees (or both). "That is clearly happening today as the younger generation demands that they won't buy anything online if they can't see how other customers have rated it," says Dan. "On the employee side, it's critically important for employees, particularly in large enterprises, to be able to find knowledge. It is not about building a database of knowledge or formal learning programs. It's the informal learning you do face-to-face or—now that more companies are distributed globally or employees working virtually—the ability to find the people in the organization who know things."

Thanks to the Web and now the social web, work styles have changed significantly and continue to evolve. Many more people are working from home or working flexible hours, and discussion forums, instant messaging, and Wikis make that possible. Employees can be productive around the clock and around the world, interacting with the associates with whom they need to consult. This trend is picking up speed as smaller gadgets and faster technologies become commonplace.

In a business context, marketing to the social web internally is a way to do something sophisticated senior managers have advocated for years: breach the silos. Ideally, no one should work in a marketing silo or a sales silo or an operations silo, but have contact with and easy access to everybody in the organization. People can work together to accomplish their goals without regard for the exact organizational structure.

Dan gives an example from his experience at Mzinga: "We have a discussion forum where our customer support people on the front lines can post questions and our engineering or marketing teams or others have access to the questions and can respond. The support people can provide better, more authoritative, and thoughtful answers by tapping the knowledge of the entire company. It's not as though everybody in the company has to sit and read every message. That doesn't happen, because people have other jobs. But it just sort of naturally works."

Also, naturally, the social web affects all other media.

Where Is Television Going?

I asked my friend Stuart Brotman how he thought the social web would affect television and radio. Stuart—the CEO of American Television Experience and past president of the Museum of Television & Radio—thinks that in 10 years, no one will be talking about the Web as a separate medium. "It will be an integral part of media, but it will not be broken out as it is today," he tells me. "We will have a term called 'television,' but television, in fact, may incorporate the Web as a concept. I don't think the Web as a whole is going to subsume television."

Stuart believes that video programming will continue to be delivered through broadcast, cable, and fiber optic. Television will continue to be a mass medium, but there will *also* be a mass medium delivered through the Internet. *How* content is delivered will not be important. Remember that most people make no distinction between a cable channel and a broadcast channel. When they watch television, they usually don't consider whether they're watching cable or something else—a situation that has important implications for the social web.

"I think the transmission infrastructure will be transparent to the user," says Stuart, "particularly as the computer becomes an integral part of the home entertainment unit. Whatever comes in on the Internet can immediately get transmitted to a home receiver in a living room, which we now know as a television set." This is already happening. A good example is Apple TV, which transmits rented or purchased programs and movies from the computer directly to the television set. "Clearly we see the beginning of the evolution of content coming off the Internet and not staying on what we know as a computer screen today, but being transmitted to another environment," he adds.

Think about how people record content off television, manipulate it, transform it (or not), and put it up on YouTube. This traffic—professionals putting out content, amateurs manipulating it and creating their own—is going both ways and will only increase. It's a great time to be an intellectual property lawyer as organizations try to defend their content.

Other companies may decide for strategic purposes that they want to have their material disseminated as widely as possible, but still within the framework of the intellectual property system. Copyright holders are making these kinds of decisions today and will face even more such decisions in the future.

The other issue, of course, is privacy. Marketers want to find out as much as possible about individuals to target their messages as narrowly as possible. Yet many consumers are uncomfortable with a company tracking their online behavior. Facebook dropped its Beacon program, which automatically told people in a user's group about the user's purchases on other sites. Charter dropped its plan to track and sell the surfing patterns of its broadband subscribers. These and other incidents attracted the attention of the U.S. Senate Commerce, Science and Transportation Committee, which last year began looking at online advertising and possible privacy violations. To my mind, the issue seems to be one of transparency and the ability to opt-in rather than, as in the Charter case, an obscure way to opt-out.

In-Home Goes Out-of-Home

These changes mean marketers must rethink how they use media. Marketers typically have been organized vertically. They've considered how much to spend on radio . . . how much on broadcast television . . . how much on cable television . . . how much on Internet advertising. Now, Stuart Brotman says, "I think a lot of those vertical categories will become more blurred, which poses opportunities and challenges for marketers. It means companies will have more discretion to break down those individual budgets and allocate them. It also means there will be higher risk factors, particularly as attempts are made to develop suitable metrics. How will you be able to measure the effectiveness of a particular ad, with a particular transmission source and a particular receiving device? Measurement will be even more complicated as the lines between in-home usage and out-of-home usage begin to dissolve."

Most marketing messages have been created to be heard or seen (or both) either outside the home, such as on car radios or billboards, or in the home, mainly on television. Increasingly, people are carrying smart phones and other devices to be in contact with the Web continuously and seamlessly from anywhere. This means marketers will have to design messages suitable for in-home and out-of-home exposure simultaneously.

Stuart gives this example: Right now, radio is a short-burst medium organized around 10-, 15-, 20-, 30-, and 60-second commercials. But marketing to the social web isn't organized that way. People sit in front of their computers for three or four hours a day linking into various web sites, sending and receiving e-mail, and checking archival material. Their involvement is clearly not governed by any particular time or period.

"The out-of-home experience is primarily these bursting messages, which are highly passive," says Stuart. "They're just thrown at you. But with devices that allow people to take the in-home experience out of home, marketers have to consider how consumers are managing their time and mobility."

With mass-market mobile media devices coming into the mainstream, we're trying to get a sense of exactly how people use them and what that means for marketing strategy. Do they use the device to get a short burst of information or do they use it for long periods of time? If you've seen commuters use their phones on a one-hour train ride instead of reading a newspaper or book or listening to an audio book or CD, you know what I mean. It becomes an hour of experience as opposed to getting the latest headlines, the sports scores, the weather.

Obviously, there's a big difference between being interrupted by a commercial and actively seeking information. If consumers want to know about flat screen television, they want to know as much as possible. There's no comparison between the information they can get from, say, a 30-second Panasonic television commercial and the detailed product specifications and reviews available on the Web. Yet both may be valuable to consumers, for different reasons.

Take Panasonic as an example. Obviously Panasonic should have broad and deep information available on its web site, including video demonstrations and specs, reviews, and all the richness of the Web.

Suppose I'm out (with a mobile device) and want to access the Best Buy or Circuit City or *Consumer Reports* site to see the five best-rated flat screen television sets. Once I get online and look at a list of the five best models, I can visit a store to see each model. I might then go home to think things over before returning to the store or ordering the chosen model online. My point is that there's likely to be interaction between that short bit of information consumers get in the mobile environment and the longer, deeper information they get in the stationary environment.

In the near future, for instance, I might have the list of five best-rated flat screen televisions on my cell phone when I visit the store. I'll be able to transmit that information to my home or office computer so when I turn the computer on or do a Google search, a special marketing system automatically delivers the Panasonic information I'm interested in. And how does the system know I'm interested? Because I was asking about such products when I was in a store.

Once you understand the pattern between stationary use (at-home or in-office) and mobile use, Stuart notes, there are creative strategies you can capitalize on. Rather than developing two different types of marketing messages, you can make them part of a system. The current marketing media system has short bursts of information, which are largely passive, as well as torrents of information, which are largely interactive. "The challenge will be: How do you mesh those two together?" Stuart asks. "Part of the answer will be based on how consumers use their devices and part will be based on how marketers condition consumers to use the devices. These are clearly dynamic processes and marketers can play a role in shaping how those usage patterns get developed."

Where Are Newspapers Going?

I'm not sure whether newspapers, as we know them, will survive. Here are just three quick symptoms of the industry's difficulties:

1. The McClatchy Company bought the *Minneapolis Star Tribune* in 1998 for $1.2 billion. Eight years later, McClatchy sold the paper to a private equity group for just $530 million. As David Carr wrote in the *New York Times*, "the consolidation of department stores and the flight of classified ads to the Web hurt big metropolitan dailies like the *Star Tribune*."[2]

2. *The Washington Post* named Marcus W. Brauchli, a *Wall Street Journal* editor, to become the executive editor of the *Post* and to help "meld its print and online news operation—something the *Journal* has already done.... The two operations have been kept apart to a degree that is rare in the industry—the Web site even has a separate newsroom, in Virginia—which has bred duplication and turf wars." The *Post*'s publisher said that Brauchli's experience at the *Journal* would "help us navigate the new world of media."[3]

3. A recent study by the Pew Research Center's Project for Excellence in Journalism found 85 percent of large daily newspapers have cut newsroom staffs in the last three years, with more cuts to come. Two thirds of all dailies have reduced space for international news, arts criticism, and science coverage.[4]

I talked to my friend Jerry Swerling about the future of print journalism and the relationship between print and the social web. Jerry, professor of professional practice at the Annenberg School for Communication at USC Los Angeles, told me: "The problem with print journalism is that they have come to believe that they are in the printing business. The business they're really in is the gathering, interpretation, and distribution of news and information. It's a distribution problem, it's a distribution opportunity, and they're hung-up on the platform."

Jerry asks rhetorically: When you think about the information-intensive age in which we live, what could be more valuable? What greater asset could you have than a large group of well-trained information-gatherers, hunters, distributors? That's a tremendously valuable asset for news organizations to have, yet leveraging that core asset is tricky. How do you distribute it? What is the model? I agree with Jerry when he says, "I don't think anybody has quite figured that one out yet."

What intrigued me was Jerry's example of how print journalism and marketing on the social web may complement one another. "In the automotive section of this morning's *Los Angeles Times*, I noticed that a reporter had written a great review of the latest BMW motorcycle. The review was followed by a couple of lines that said, in effect, 'By the way, not satisfied with what you see on the page, go to such and such a link and you can see video of the reporter testing the bike. Go along with her.' That's brilliant."

Jerry followed the link and found that readers can comment on the *Times* review and the pros and cons of the BMW bike versus the traditional Triumph or Harley Davidson bikes. It's a wonderful blend of social networking and journalism. The reporter, he says, "is building a community, in a sense, around her experience and her expertise. And maybe that's the direction in which journalism will have to go: Build a community around your reporters' areas of expertise and create a more personal connection between the reader, the viewer, the consumer."

I can definitely see a role for marketers in this kind of situation. Shouldn't BMW (and Triumph and Harley Davidson and Kawasaki) be part of this discussion? I can see BMW participating in a dialogue to which it would otherwise never have had access. BMW engineers could, for example, explain why they designed the controls or the suspension in a certain way. To be more specific, suppose the reporter's review said, "There was one thing I didn't like about this bike: the transmission isn't as smooth as it could be." A consumer might respond and say, "That's been my problem, too, but it's still a big improvement over the last BMW model." At that point, BMW has a golden opportunity to chime in and say, "Let us tell you why we made that change."

Where is the Social Web Going?

Forrester Research's analysts have made several predictions of where social computing (their term for the social web) is heading. Here's what Charlene Li, Jeremiah Owyang, and Peter Kim think:

Corporate participation will bring social applications to the mainstream. Companies will move beyond one-off experiments in social media to establish full-fledged initiatives. Online marketing campaigns will sponsor communities, post YouTube videos, establish social networking groups, and create widgets, further pushing adoption by mainstream consumers. Early adopter purists will leave for ad-free zones, but Forrester says they'll be replaced by ordinary consumers testing the waters because their friends and the companies they trust have shown that social applications are not only safe, but fun and useful.

Community manager roles will gain prominence in companies. As companies realize how important social applications are to their marketing and business strategies, formal budgets and roles will become more standard in large marketing organizations. These executives may not all have the same title, but they will share similar duties and responsibilities: to develop a social web strategy and start to deploy social tools and programs for marketing.

Corporate social responsibility will take on a new meaning. Between fake blogs and flat marketer profiles on social networks that shout at—rather than talk with—site members, companies have not been at their best on the social web. Moreover, consumers have become more vocal about preserving control over their information and experiences. (Privacy again.)

Customer needs will gain a voice. Traditional marketing starts with companies pitching to prospects. More and more, customers will state their intention to buy products or services via a Web-based marketplace. eBay's "Want It Now" program will get a boost when the company turns the existing bulletin board/announcement service into a bidding-based marketplace. It's possible that college students on Facebook will organize buying clubs centered on an entire dormitory, allowing marketers to move bulk merchandise with a single purchase order.

Micromedia adoption will increase, and marketers will learn to join in. Twitter, Powce, Jaiku, Utterz, and other microblogging and micromedia tools give users the opportunity to share short sentences or audio clips with trusted friends. Better search and aggregation tools, as well as the ability to have differentiated, group-based distribution, will make these micromedia conversations more useful and relevant.

The social graph (meaning a map of the connections and relationships between people) will open up. Social network members are asking for the ability to express their personal social profiles across multiple sites, for example, on both Facebook and LinkedIn.

Social search will make its debut by re-ranking search results based on inputs from your personalized search history as well as the searching patterns of your social graph. For example, people with similar searching patterns and people like you within your social networks might favor a particular site over others in a search for "china." If so, that link will move up higher in the results. Sites like Collarity, Eurekster, Mahalo, Wink Technologies, and Wikia Search are currently edging into this area. As a result, search engine optimization and even "social media optimization" will not have as much impact because individual and group behaviors will be nearly impossible to manipulate. Marketers will have to focus their efforts instead on meeting the specific needs of targeted personas, building a following, and critical mass to eventually influence the social rankings of their web sites.[5]

This Is Only the Beginning

You have to understand the landscape to make sense of it, and it's clear that the landscape of the social web is changing almost daily. Volcanoes are erupting (Google, Facebook, MySpace, YouTube), sinkholes are developing, there are swamps and deserts. Legal and ethical issues such as copyright infringement and privacy are evolving and many areas are, at this writing, grey rather than black and white. The social web is having a major impact, but different industries are going to be affected differently.

Think about how the Web disrupted the music industry and the travel industry, says Judy Strauss, associate professor of marketing at the University of Nevada, Reno. As the whole landscape changed, established firms like Tower Records went out of business and hundreds of travel agents went under.

"The traditional mainstream media industry has this huge disruption," Judy observes. "They're now competing with bloggers for advertising dollars and with the social web for eyeballs," Judy observes. "As users, we want to read whatever is relevant to our particular interests. As a user, I'll go where people are talking about what I'm interested in. In many cases, videos posted by users are more relevant to me than what the media outlets are posting."

Perhaps a constraint on this change is the lack of bandwidth. Despite the fact that half of all U.S. households have broadband access, significant changes like being able to quickly download high-definition television shows will not become commonplace without more bandwidth.

As I mentioned earlier in this chapter, the social web is already affecting television and newspapers. It's certainly having an effect on the advertising industry and will probably change the movie industry. (What happens when a million young people make their own short movies and post them on YouTube? When you can download any movie from the Netflix library?) Looking ahead, will financial services be the next industry to be disrupted? Or insurance? Or health care?

I don't pretend to have the answers—but stay tuned because (as I said at the beginning of the book) the social web isn't just a channel or another medium for marketing messages. In effect, it's becoming the closest thing to physical life. This is very important because, whether you're a small company with a chain of restaurants or a giant corporation with a global presence, you're going to have to start talking to customers and prospects as if they were with you in the room.

You'll have to create communities through content, through visual impact, and through conversation, and allow friends and strangers to share their thoughts—the good, the bad, and the truly ugly—about your products, your offers, your sales, your weaknesses, your strengths. Through openness, transparency, and truth you can live and thrive on the social web until the Web and marketing disappear.

NOTES

Chapter 1

1. "Lenovo's Web Marketer: Twittering's Not for Twits," Brandweek .com, May 11, 2008, www.brandweek.com.
2. See http://www.ning.com/?view=search&term=IBM.
3. See http://h18004.www1.hp.com/products/blades/components/ bladeconnect.html?jumpid=reg_R1002_USEN and http://forums 12.itrc.hp.com/service/forums/home.do?admit=109447627 +1213110531389+28353475.
4. See http://www.kayakmind.com/.
5. Steve Lohr, "Is Windows Near End of Its Run?" *New York Times*, October 14, 2006, p. C3.
6. Michael Bush, "Linking Web Buzz to Mini Sales," *Advertising Age*, May 19, 2008, p. 4.
7. Kevin J. Delaney, Emily Steel, and Vauhini Vara, "Social Sites Don't Deliver Big Ad Gains," *Wall Street Journal*, February 5, 2008, p. B1.
8. Bruce D. Temkin and Ross Popoff-Walker, "Young Gen Yers: Fun-loving, Social, and Wired," Forrester Market Research, January 3, 2008.
9. David Kesmodel and John R. Wilke, "Whole Foods Is Hot, Wild Oats a Dud—So Said 'Rahodeb,'" *Wall Street Journal*, July 12, 2007, p. A1.
10. Jenn Abelson, "CEO Tells the Whole Story," *Boston Globe*, May 21, 2008, www.boston.com.

Chapter 2

1. Heather Green, "It Takes a Web Village: Private Online Communities Are Providing Special Insights into Customers' Needs," *BusinessWeek*, September 4, 2006, p. 66.
2. Jonathan Lucas, "Stealth Marketing Hits SoNo Scene," *Stamford Advocate*, June 17, 2007.
3. "About BabyCenter" page, www.babycenter.com.

Chapter 3

1. Justin Martin, "How Intuit Boosts Sales," Fortune Small Business, May 27, 2008, http://money.cnn.com/galleries/2008/fsb/0805/gallery.nps_success_stories.fsb/.
2. Hiawatha Bray, "A 'Bold' Step to Fix Ford's Image," *Boston Globe*, September 7, 2006, p. E.1.

Chapter 4

1. http://www.complaints.com/2008/april/29/Ford___Volvo_168825.htm.
2. Bradford Wernle, "Leaked message is not RX for Mazda; Private telecast shows up on Web." Automotive News, August 14, 2006, p. 3.
3. http://www.rx8club.com/showthread.php?p=2495847#post2495847, http://www.rx8club.com/showthread.php?t=147287.
4. Shankar Gupta, "Jeff Jarvis vs. Dell: Blogger's Complaint Becomes Viral Nightmare." http://publications.mediapost.com/index.cfm?fuseaction=Articles.showArticleHomePage&art_aid=33307
5. Pete Blackshaw, "Lessons from Jeff Jarvis + Dell." http://notetaker.typepad.com/cgm/2005/08/lessons_from_je.html.
6. "Measuring the Influence of Bloggers on Corporate Reputation," December 2005 http://www.onalytica.com/MeasuringBloggerInfluence61205.pdf.
7. Dan Fost, "On the Internet, Everyone Can Hear You Complain," *New York Times*, February 25, 2008, p. C6.

8. "Bloggers FAQ—Online Defamation Law." http://www.eff.org/bloggers/lg/faq-defamation.php.

9. Mark Sweney, "Should Stealth Marketing Be Regulated?" The Guardian, May 21, 2008, http://blogs.guardian.co.uk/organgrinder/2008/05/should_commercial_blogging_be.html.

10. Jonathan Fahey, "Candid Camera: Damage Control in the Age of You Tube." http://www.forbes.com/archive/forbes/2006/1113/124.html.

Chapter 5

1. "Growing Number Of Japanese Writing Blogs On The Internet." AsiaPulse News (Jan 28, 2008): NA.

Chapter 6

1. "North American Social Technographis Online Survey," Forrester Research, January 7, 2008.

2. Survey quoted in Forrester Research study, Interactive Marketing Data Overview, US 2007, February 26, 2008, p. 3.

3. Faves.com survey quoted in Elisabeth A. Sullivan, "Be Sociable," Marketing News, January 15, 2008, p. 15.

4. "S-Commerce: Beyond MySpace and YouTube," Spark, October 2006, p. 5, www.compete.inc.com/research/spark.

5. "Lego Ambassadors." http://www.lego.com/eng/info/default.asp?page=ambassadors.

Chapter 7

1. "Vertical Search—Welcome to the Next Generation of Search," Revolution, April 1, 2008, p. 56.

2. Jefferson Graham, "Google's Cutts: Good directions drive traffic to your website," USA Today, June 22, 2008; http://www.usatoday.com/tech/products/services/2008-06-22-google-search-engine-optimization_N.htm.

3. Peggy Anne Salz, "NMA Mobile: Search Pattern," *New Media Age*, May 8, 2008. p. 26.
4. Stefan Stern, "Word on the Blog Says Sun King Rules," *Daily Telegraph*, May 1, 2006, p. 1.
5. Jim White, "How the salesmen hijacked YouTube," http://www.telegraph.co.uk/opinion/main.jhtml?xml=/opinion/2008/06/16/do1602.xml.

Chapter 8

1. Ellen Lee, "Social Sites Becoming Too Much of a Good Thing," San Francisco Chronicle, November 2, 2006, http://www.sfgate.com/cgi-bin/article.cgi?f=/c/a/2006/11/02/MNGG3M4KB31.DTL&hw=Social+Sites+Becoming+Too+Much+of+Good+Thing&sn=010&sc=453.
2. http://www.communispace.com/3_news/press_releases/pr_100406.asp.
3. http://www.tns-mi.com/news/03252008.htm.

Chapter 9

1. "Social Media Monitoring and Analysis," Aberdeen Group, January 2008, p.8.
2. Ibid.
3. Brian Haven and Suresh Vittal, "Measuring Engagement" Forrester Research, June 10, 2008; also Brian Haven, "Marketing's New Key Metric: Engagement," Forrester Research, August 8, 2007.
4. Rene Algesheimer and Paul M. Dholakia, "Do Customer Communities Pay Off?" *Harvard Business Review*, November 2006, p. 26.

Chapter 10

1. Elisabeth A. Sullivan, "H.J. Heinz Company," *Marketing News*, February 1, 2008, p. 10.

2. Kathleen M. Joyce, "Motivating Out of the Box," *Promo*, November 1, 2006.

Chapter 11

1. The Friendster story is based on Gary Rivlin, "Wallflower at the Web Party," New York Times, October 15, 2006, sec.3, p. 1; Steve Rosenbush, "Why MySpace Is the Hot Place," BusinessWeek Online, May 31, 2005; "Friendster Tries for a Comeback," *InternetWeek*, May 19, 2006.
2. "MySpace Received 76 Percent of U.S Social Networking Visits in 2007," Hitwise news release, January 16, 2008, hitwise.com.
3. "SEO: What is It? Do I Need it? http://tcwebsite.com/demo2/resources/case-studies.
4. "Privacy Policy." http://coachandrea.com/html/privacy_policy.html.
5. Nevertheless, I titled my first book, *The Provocateur: How a New Generation of Leaders Are Building Communities, Not Just Companies* (New York: Crown Business, 2001).

Chapter 12

1. "Nielsen Online Announces May U.S. Search Share Rankings," June 19, 2008, www.nielsen-online.com.
2. Deborah Fallows, "Search Engine Users," Pew Internet & American Life Project, http://www.pewInternet.org/pdfs/PIP_Searchengine_users.pdf.
3. Steve Miller, "Google: Organic Results, Plus Paid, Will Pay Off," *Brandweek*, December 10, 2007, p. 11.
4. Timothy Daly, "We're Number Two," *Multichannel Merchant*, June 1, 2006.
5. Ralph F. Wilson, "Organic Search versus Paid Search," Web Marketing Today Free Weekly, http://www.wilsonweb.com/paid-search/organic-paid.htm.

6. Justin Yates, "Letter: Niche Terms Are the Key to Paid Search," *New Media Age*, December 6, 2007, p. 17.
7. "Paid Search Faces Up to Social Media," *Revolution*, March 14, 2008, p. 57.
8. Carol Krol, "Search Draws Big Spending," *B to B*, March 24, 2008, p. 19.
9. Miguel Helft, "The Retooling of a Search Engine," *New York Times*, December 4, 2006,
10. Mark Roth, "The Thinkers: An Engine that 'Does Search Right,'" Pittsburgh Post-Gazette, June 26, 2006. http://www.post-gazette.com/pg/pp06177/701252.stm

Chapter 13

1. Wikipedia, "blog," http://en.wikipedia.org/wiki (accessed December 20, 2006).
2. Paul Gillin, "New Influencers," http://www.gillin.com/NISurvey.htm.
3. https://estranet.edelman.com/bloggerstudy
4. Edelman Trust Barometer 2008, p. 14.
5. Stephen Baker and Heather Green, "Beyond Blogs," *Business Week*, June 2, 2008, pp. 45–50.
6. Allison Enright, "Brill's Blog Builds Community and Gets it Right," *Marketing News*, December 15, 2005, p. 23.
7. IBMers' blogs, http://www.ibm.com/blogs/zz/en/.
8. Oliver Ryan, "Blogger in Chief," *Fortune*, November 13, 2006, p. 51.
9. Stefan Stern, "Word on the Blog Says Sun King Rules," http://www.telegraph.co.uk.
10. Nancy Mann Jackson, "State of Blogging," *State Legislatures*, May 2008, pp. 30+.
11. Marianne Aiello, "In a Sea of Controversy, Blogs Can Be Life Rafts," *Healthcare Marketing Advisor*, July 2008, pp. 10+.
12. http://www.sun.com/aboutsun/media/blogs/policy.html.
13. http://www.sun.com/rss/podcast.html.

Chapter 14

1. Jerry Adlere, "Fast Chat: Starting a New Slate," *Newsweek*, July 3, 2006, p. 16.
2. Paul, Pamela, "Healthy Babies Need Irony," *New York Times*, December 10, 2006, S.9, p. 2.
3. Stuart Elliott, "A Meet-Up, Brought to You by Huggies," *New York Times*, March 19, 2008, p. C6.
4. Claire Cain Miller, "The New Back Fence," *Forbes*, April 7, 2008, p. 66.

Chapter 15

1. "YouTube's Dominance of Web Video Grows," *InformationWeek*, June 26, 2008.
2. Robert D. Putnam, *Bowling Alone: The Collapse and Revival of American Community* (New York: Simon & Schuster, 1995), p. vii.
3. Randall Stross, "Do Boomers Want a Web Home of Their Own?" *New York Times*, February 10, 2008, p. 4.
4. Michael Arrington, "Ning Worth Half a Billion Dollars," Techcrunch, April 18, 2008, www.techcrunch.com/2008/04/18/ning-worth-half-a-billion-dollars/.
5. Adam L. Penenberg, "Ning's Infinite Ambition," Fast Company, April 11, 2008, www.fastcompany.com/magazine/125/nings-infinite-ambition.html.

Chapter 16

1. David Wilkins, "How Workplace Communities will Transform Your Business," Mzinga white paper, (www.mzinga.com), January 2008, p. 4.
2. http://www.techcrunch.com/wp-content/facebookdemographic.png
3. http://news.cnet.com/8301-13577_3-9973826-36.html?tag=bl
4. http://www.comscore.com/press/release.asp?press=1519

5. Greg Andersen, "Marketers, Don't Just Blindly Follow Latest Media Trends," *Advertising Age*, June 2, 2008, p. 20.
6. Patricia R. Olsen, "The Old Family Tea Business Gets a New-Media Spin," *New York Times*, May 31, 2008, p. C2.
7. Stuart Elliott. "For Coors Light, a Night Out That Begins on MySpace." *New York Times*, May 28, 2008, p. C6.
8. Christina Rexrode, "Your Bank. Also Your Facebook Friend?" *Charlotte Observer*, June 9, 2008.

Chapter 17

1. Stuart Elliott, "Letting Consumers Control Marketing: Priceless," *New York Times*, October 9, 2006, p. C8.
2. David Carr, "The Lonely Newspaper Reader," *New York Times*, January 1, 2007, p. C1.
3. Richard Pérez-Peña, "Washington Post Signals Shift With a New Editor," *New York Times*, July 8, 2008, p. C3.
4. Mark Fitzgerald, "After Layoffs: Newspapers Get Smaller, Pew Study Finds," Editor & Publisher, http://www.editorandpublisher.com/eandp/news/article_display.jsp?vnu_content_id=1003829623.
5. Charlene Li, Jeremiah Owyang, and Peter Kim, "Top Social Computing Predictions for 2008," Forrester Research, January 15, 2008, pp. 1–3.

INDEX